healthy everyday

High Fiber

healthy everyday

High Fiber

70 delicious recipes designed with nutrition in mind

Introduction

We all lead busy lives, and it can sometimes be hard to keep on top of healthy habits, with fiber often dropping out of our priorities. However, having plenty of fiber in our diets is associated with many health benefits, so these fiber-rich recipes are designed to increase our fiber intake—without compromising on flavor.

What Is Fiber?

The term fiber (or roughage, as it was once called) describes not just one but a number of carbohydrates found in the cell walls of plants. For many years, we believed its only role was to provide bulk to the stools, but new research suggests it does much more than that.

Unlike other carbohydrates, fiber can't be broken down by the digestive enzymes, so it ends up in the large intestine where it's broken down by gut bacteria, creating short-chain fatty acids. Short-chain fatty acids nourish the cells in the colon, help to reduce inflammation, and encourage the growth of "friendly" bacteria, which research suggests offer various health benefits above and beyond gut health.

Different types of fiber help keep the body healthy in different ways. Insoluble fiber, found in foods like wheat bran, vegetables, and whole grains, helps food move through the digestive system and provides bulk to the stools, making them softer and easier to pass. Soluble fiber, found in oats, beans and pulses, and some fruits and vegetables, dissolves to form a thick paste in the stomach, which binds to sugars and cholesterol, helping to lower blood cholesterol levels and slow the absorption of sugar.

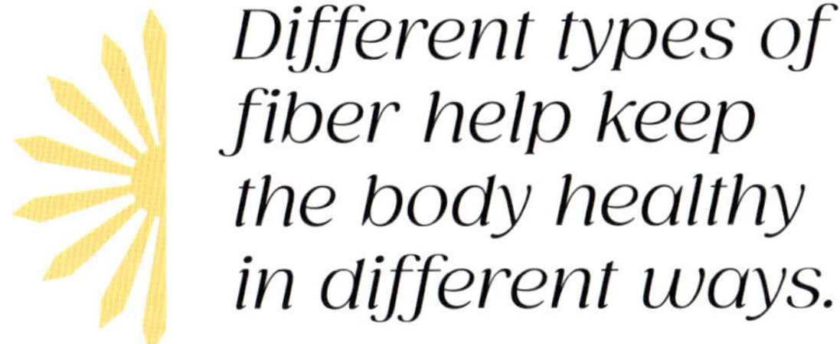

Different types of fiber help keep the body healthy in different ways.

The Health Benefits of Fiber

Fiber is beneficial to the body in many ways, reducing the risk of some illnesses and improving your overall health. A fiber-rich diet can:

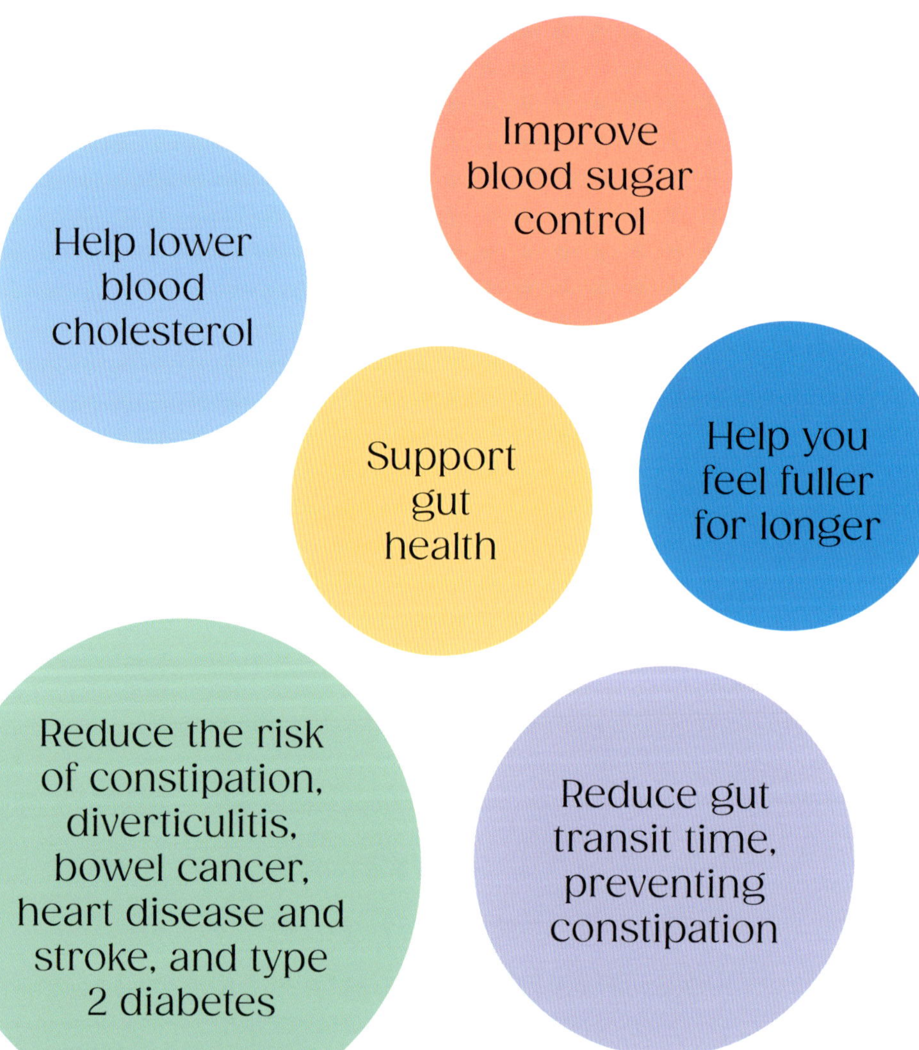

Some types of fiber, particularly inulin, fructo-oligosaccharides (FOS), and galacto-oligosaccharides (GOS), provide food for good (probiotic) bacteria in the gut. Known as prebiotics, they're found in some fruits, vegetables, nuts, grains, and pulses, highlighting the importance of eating a variety of plants.

How Much Fiber Do We Need?

The recommended intake for fiber varies around the world. The US recommendation is 28g per day, whereas the World Health Organization (WHO) recommends 25g of fiber per day for adults. The WHO guidelines are:

Age group	Recommended daily intake
Adults	25g/day
Children 10 years and over	25g/day
Children 6–9 years	21g/day
Children 2–5 years	15g/day

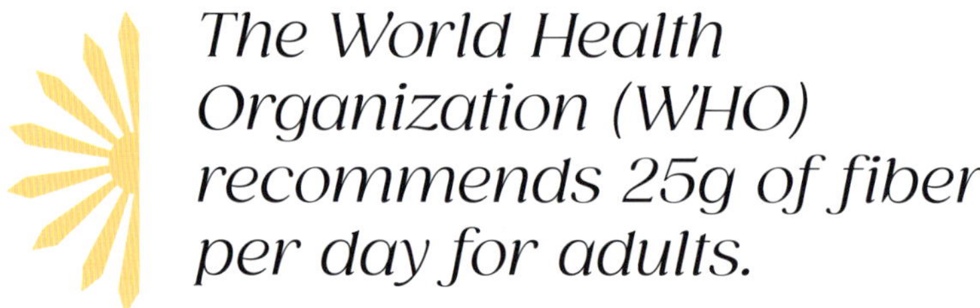

The World Health Organization (WHO) recommends 25g of fiber per day for adults.

How to Increase Your Fiber Intake

There are plenty of ways you can add more fiber to your diet in order to reach your fiber goal:

* **Choose whole grain cereal**, such as bran flakes, oatmeal, or muesli, at breakfast. A medium-sized bowl of bran flakes plus a chopped banana will get your day off to a good start, making it easier to reach your daily target.

* **Add beans and pulses** to soups, casseroles, and salads. Canned beans are a great source of soluble fiber, are just as nutritious as dried beans, and are a good pantry ingredient. Rinse canned beans well to remove sugars that can cause wind.

* **Eat at least five servings** of fruits and vegetables a day. Fruit and vegetables contain both soluble and insoluble fiber. Much of the fiber is present in the skin, so whenever possible, don't peel them.

* **Eat dried fruits**, such as apricots or prunes, as a snack, or add them to your breakfast cereal.

* **Use whole wheat flour** for baking—weight for weight, whole wheat flour contains three times as much fiber as white flour and significantly higher levels of several of the B vitamins.

* **Choose whole wheat** or multigrain bread rather than white. Although white bread does contain some fiber, whole wheat contains four times as much. If you don't like whole wheat, look for fiber-enriched white bread.

* **Eat beans** on whole wheat toast for lunch. This quick and healthy snack will provide over half of the recommended daily fiber intake.

* **Choose brown rice** and whole wheat pasta, rather than white.

* **Eat the skin** of your baked potato—baked potatoes eaten along with their skin have twice as much fiber as those without.

* **Boost the fiber** content of dishes like shepherd's pie and spaghetti bolognese by adding a can of brown lentils.

* **Swap cookies** for a fiber-rich cereal bar.

* **Choose lentil soup** rather than chicken soup. Tuscan bean soup, minestrone soup, and vegetable soup also provide good amounts of fiber.

* **Boost the fiber** content of sandwiches by adding coleslaw or grated carrot.

Tips and Tricks

Equipment

Having the right equipment on hand can make it much simpler to whip up high-fiber recipes at home. Here are a few handy things to have in the kitchen:

* **An air fryer** is very useful for cooking tasty, fiber-packed snacks in a hurry, such as celery root fries (see p129), sweet potato wedges (see p134), or pakoras (see p137). It is cost-effective and quick to use and ensures delicious, crispy results.

* **Large pots and pans** are essential for batch-cooking recipes to fill up the freezer.

* **Storage containers** are useful for those batch-cooked meals. Having healthy meals on hand means that you always have a high-fiber option when time is short.

Hacks

Here are a few tips and tricks to make following a high-fiber diet easier:

* **Meal planning** by following the planner on pages 16–17 will ensure you balance the amount of fiber you're getting in each meal. It can also help you do one big shop for the week and avoid doing emergency dashes to the supermarket or falling back on less nutritious options.

* **Filling the pantry and freezer** with easy fiber-packed options, such as canned beans and lentils, frozen vegetables and berries, oats and grains, bags of nuts and seeds, and pouches of microwaveable grains, means you'll always have the basics to be able to rustle something up.

Meal Planner

Planning your meals for the week ahead, taking into account the fiber content per portion, which is provided at the top of each recipe, is a clever way to achieve your fiber goals.

	MONDAY	TUESDAY	WEDNESDAY
BREAKFAST	Breakfast Smoothie (see p20) **Fiber per serving: 6.5g**		
LUNCH	Lemony Butternut Squash and Quinoa Salad (see p52) **Fiber per serving: 10g**		
DINNER	Eggplant Ragù with Bean Mash (see p114) **Fiber per serving: 19g**		
SNACKS & SWEETS	Carrot Cake Bites (see p164) **Fiber per serving: 3g**		
DAILY FIBER COUNT	**Total Fiber: 38.5g**		

THURSDAY	FRIDAY	SATURDAY	SUNDAY

Breakfast

Starting your day with a high-fiber breakfast is always a good idea. These recipes have been designed to help you enjoy the usual breakfast treats, such as fluffy pancakes or delicious soda bread, but in a healthier way, by choosing nutritious whole grain options.

Breakfast Smoothie

Kcals 260
Protein 6g
Fiber 6.5g

Serves 2

Prep time: 5 minutes

- 4 pitted dates
- 3 kiwifruits, peeled and roughly chopped
- 1 apple, cored and roughly chopped
- large handful of spinach
- ½ in (1 cm) piece of ginger, peeled and roughly chopped
- 3 tbsp old-fashioned rolled oats
- 1 cup (200 ml) water
- ice cubes

1 To a high speed blender, add in all the ingredients. Blend until smooth, then divide between two glasses.

Tip This green smoothie is a great way to get energized, while also getting your greens in, early in the day.

Kiwifruits are a great source of vitamin C. They are also rich in the phytochemical lutein, which helps protect your eyes from damage from sunlight.

Granola

Kcals 443
Protein 11g
Fiber 6.5g

Serves 8

Prep + cook time: 40 minutes

- 2½ cups (250g) old-fashioned rolled oats
- ⅓ cup (50g) sunflower seeds
- ⅓ cup (50g) pumpkin seeds
- 1 cup (150g) mixed nuts (such as walnut halves, hazelnuts, or almonds), roughly chopped
- ½ cup (70g) pitted dates, roughly chopped
- 2 tsp ground cinnamon
- 2 tsp ground ginger
- ½ tsp salt
- 3 tbsp vegetable oil
- 3 tbsp maple syrup
- 1 cup (50g) coconut flakes

1 Preheat the oven to 350°F (180°C).

2 To a large bowl, add the oats, sunflower seeds, pumpkin seeds, nuts, dates, cinnamon, ginger, salt, vegetable oil, and maple syrup. Mix well.

3 Divide the mixture between two large baking sheets and spread out evenly. Cook for 20 minutes, stirring occasionally.

4 Add the coconut flakes and cook for a further 10 minutes until golden. Let cool.

Keep it Store in an airtight container for up to 2 weeks.

Oats are rich in beta-glucans, a type of soluble fiber that can help reduce high cholesterol and keep blood sugar levels stable.

Oatmeal with Cherries

Kcals 265
Protein 8g
Fiber 3.5g

Serves 2

Prep + cook time: 15 minutes

- 3½ oz (100g) frozen cherries
- 1 tbsp maple syrup, plus extra to serve
- ½ tsp ground ginger
- ½ cup (60g) old-fashioned rolled oats
- ⅔ cup (150ml) milk
- ⅔ cup (150ml) water
- ½ tsp ground cinnamon
- 1 tbsp sunflower seeds

1 To a small saucepan, add the cherries, maple syrup, and ground ginger. Add a splash of water, then set over low-medium heat. Cover and cook for 5 minutes until the cherries have burst and softened. Set aside.

2 To a large saucepan, add the oats, milk, and water. Set over low-medium heat and cook for about 10 minutes, stirring continuously, until thick and creamy.

3 Divide the oatmeal between two bowls, top with the cherries, drizzle over some extra maple syrup, and sprinkle over the cinnamon and sunflower seeds.

Swap it To keep this recipe even more simple, leave out the cherries, and serve the oatmeal simply with a drizzle of maple syrup.

Protein from the oats is vital for promoting strong bone and muscle function, while the addition of cherries and seeds increases the quantity of fiber.

Açaí Bowl

Kcals 387
Protein 10g
Fiber 12g

Serves 2

Prep time: 5 minutes

- 14oz (400g) frozen mixed berries
- 1 banana
- 1 tbsp maple syrup
- 2 tbsp Greek yogurt
- 2 tbsp almond butter

Toppings:

- 1 banana, sliced
- 3 tbsp granola
- 1 tbsp coconut chips
- 3 tbsp berries of choice

1 To a blender, add the frozen berries, banana, maple syrup, Greek yogurt, and almond butter. Blend until smooth, then divide between two bowls.

2 Top with sliced banana, granola, coconut chips, and berries, then serve.

Tip This is the perfect summer breakfast to fuel the day with plenty of fiber.

When fresh berries aren't in season, frozen berries are a good alternative. Vitamins are locked in when they are frozen, so, like fresh berries, they are a great source of vitamin C.

Zucchini Soda Bread

Kcals 225
Protein 9g
Fiber 4g

Makes 8 slices

Prep + cook time: 1 hour

- 1⅓ cups (175g) whole wheat flour, plus extra for dusting
- 1⅓ cups (175g) all-purpose flour
- ½ tsp baking soda
- 2 tbsp sunflower seeds
- ½ cup (50g) grated Cheddar cheese
- 2 green onions, finely chopped
- 1 tbsp finely chopped rosemary
- 5½oz (150g) zucchini, grated
- 1 tsp salt
- 1¼ cups (300ml) buttermilk

1 Preheat the oven to 400°F (200°C). Line a large baking sheet with parchment paper and set aside.

2 To a large bowl, add both flours, baking soda, sunflower seeds, Cheddar cheese, green onions, rosemary, zucchini, and salt.

3 Make a well in the middle, then pour in the buttermilk and mix until you have a rough dough.

4 Sprinkle a little extra flour onto a clean surface, then tip the dough out and knead for 1 minute until it comes together as a rough ball.

5 Put the dough onto the lined baking sheet, and flatten slightly with your hand, then cut a crisscross pattern on the top of the dough.

6 Cook for 45 minutes until golden. When you tap the base of the loaf, it should sound hollow.

7 Leave to cool for 10 minutes, then serve.

Keep it This bread can be sliced and stored in the freezer for up to 3 months.

Sunflower seeds boost the fiber and protein in this bread and are a good source of vitamin E and the B vitamin folate.

Mango and Passion Fruit Overnight Oats

Kcals 383
Protein 12g
Fiber 9.5g

Serves 4

Prep time: 5 minutes, plus overnight resting

- 2 cups (200g) old-fashioned rolled oats
- 4 tbsp chia seeds
- 2 tbsp maple syrup
- 2 passion fruits, halved
- 1¾ cups (400ml) milk of choice
- 7oz (200g) mango, peeled, pitted, and roughly chopped
- 4 tbsp sunflower or pumpkin seeds (optional)

1 To a large bowl add the porridge oats, chia seeds, maple syrup, and milk. Mix well, then divide among four jars or bowls and top with the passion fruit pulp and chopped mango. Cover and leave in the fridge overnight, or up to 4 days.

2 When ready to eat, top with sunflower or pumpkin seeds, if using.

Tip These overnight oats are a great way to stay ahead of your breakfast game! Prep these in advance and thank yourself later.

Mangoes are an excellent source of vitamin C and beta-carotene, both of which help keep the skin healthy and youthful.

Buckwheat Pancakes

Kcals 506
Protein 16g
Fiber 3.5g

Serves 2

Prep + cook time: 15 minutes

- 2 tbsp (30g) unsalted butter
- ¾ cup (100g) buckwheat flour
- ¾ cup (100g) all-purpose flour
- ½ tsp salt
- 1 tsp baking powder
- 2 eggs
- 2 tbsp maple syrup, plus extra to serve
- 1¼ cups (300g) plain yogurt
- 2 tbsp vegetable oil
- 3½oz (100g) blueberries
- 3 tbsp pistachios, walnuts, or sliced almonds
- 2 tbsp Greek yogurt

1 Add the butter to a small saucepan set over low heat. Cook for a few seconds until melted, then set aside.

2 To a bowl, add both flours, the salt, baking powder, melted butter, eggs, maple syrup, and plain yogurt. Mix well, then set aside.

3 Add a little of the oil to a large nonstick skillet set over medium heat. Once hot, spoon in a few ladlefuls of the pancake mixture into the pan, making sure they are well spaced out (you may need to do this in batches). Cook for 2 minutes, then flip and cook for 2 minutes on the other side until golden and cooked through.

4 Stack the pancakes on plates, then top with the blueberries and nuts. Drizzle over a little extra maple syrup and serve with the Greek yogurt.

Swap it These would also work well with other berries or chopped bananas.

Anthocyanins (the phytochemicals that give blueberries their blue-purple color) are powerful antioxidants, linked with a number of health benefits.

Banana and Peanut Butter Muffins

Kcals	241
Protein	7g
Fiber	3g

Makes 12

Prep + cook time: 35 minutes

- 3 bananas
- ½ cup (120g) crunchy peanut butter
- 2 eggs
- ⅓ cup (100g) Greek yogurt
- ¼ cup (50ml) vegetable oil
- ½ cup (100g) soft brown sugar
- 2 cups (240g) whole wheat flour
- 2 tsp baking powder
- ½ tsp salt
- 1¾oz (50g) dark chocolate nibs (optional)

1 Preheat the oven to 400°F (200°C). Line a 12-cup muffin pan with cupcake liners, then set aside.

2 Add the bananas to a bowl and mash well with a fork. Add the peanut butter, eggs, Greek yogurt, and vegetable oil. Whisk well, then add in the sugar, flour, baking powder, and salt. Mix well until combined.

3 Divide the mixture among the cupcake liners. Press the chocolate nibs, if using, into the tops of the muffins. Bake for 25 minutes or until a skewer comes out clean.

Tip To add even more fiber, use a high-quality peanut butter, as it often contains the peanut skins.

In addition to providing fiber and healthy fats, peanut butter helps boost the protein in these sustaining muffins.

Mushrooms on Toast

Kcals 418
Protein 15g
Fiber 5.5g

Serves 2

Prep + cook time:
15 minutes

- 2 tbsp extra-virgin olive oil
- 14oz (400g) mixed mushrooms, sliced
- salt and freshly ground black pepper
- 1 shallot, finely chopped
- 1 clove of garlic, crushed
- 2 slices of multigrain or seeded sourdough bread
- 1 tbsp crème fraîche
- 1 tbsp finely chopped tarragon, plus extra to serve
- 1 tbsp finely chopped chives, plus extra to serve
- 3 tbsp pumpkin seeds

1 Add the olive oil to a large skillet set over medium-high heat. Once hot, add the mushrooms and cook for 5 minutes. Add in the shallot and garlic, season with salt and freshly ground black pepper, and cook for a further 3 minutes until the mushrooms are golden in color.

2 Meanwhile, toast the bread, then set aside.

3 Add the crème fraîche to the mushrooms, then add the tarragon and chives and stir through.

4 Spoon the creamy mushrooms on top of the toast, sprinkle over the pumpkin seeds and some extra herbs, and serve.

Tip This is the ultimate savory breakfast. Mushrooms are packed with fiber and will keep you feeling full until lunch.

Pumpkin seeds are a good source of zinc, which is important for a healthy immune system. They also contain useful amounts of iron, protein, and magnesium.

Mexican-style Eggs

Kcals 786
Protein 33g
Fiber 14g

Serves 2

Prep + cook time: 30 minutes

- 2 tbsp extra-virgin olive oil, divided
- 1 onion, finely chopped
- 2 large tomatoes, roughly chopped
- 1 cup (200g) canned black beans, drained and rinsed
- 1 tbsp chipotle en adobo
- handful of cilantro, roughly chopped
- salt and freshly ground black pepper
- ¾ cup (100g) canned corn, drained and rinsed
- 4 small flour tortillas
- 4 eggs
- 1 small avocado, mashed
- 1½oz (40g) feta
- juice of 1 lime

1 Add 1 tablespoon olive oil to a skillet set over medium heat. Once hot, add the onion and cook for 5 minutes until softened. Add in the tomatoes, black beans, chipotle en adobo, cilantro, and a splash of water. Season with salt and freshly ground black pepper, then cook for 10 minutes until the beans and tomatoes have softened.

2 Set a small skillet over high heat. Once hot, add in the sweet corn and cook for 4 minutes until charred in places, then remove and set aside.

3 Add the flour tortillas to the same pan and cook for 30 seconds on both sides until golden. Remove from the pan and divide between two plates.

4 Add the remaining tablespoon of olive oil to the same pan, and crack in the eggs. Fry for a couple of minutes until cooked.

5 Meanwhile, start building the wraps. Spoon over some of the tomato bean mixture, top with the corn and mashed avocado, add the eggs, crumble over the feta, squeeze over some lime juice, and serve.

Swap it To make this vegan, leave out the eggs and swap the feta out for a vegan cheese.

The canning process actually increases availability of the beta-carotene in sweet corn, making it easier for the body to absorb.

Pea and Spinach Frittata

Kcals 459
Protein 32g
Fiber 6.5g

Serves 2

Prep + cook time: 30 minutes

- 1 tbsp extra-virgin olive oil
- 1 onion, finely chopped
- 1 red pepper, seeded and roughly chopped
- 5 eggs
- salt and freshly ground black pepper
- 3½oz (100g) spinach, roughly chopped
- ¾ cup (100g) frozen peas
- ½ cup (50g) grated Gruyère or Cheddar cheese
- whole wheat toast, to serve (optional)

1 Preheat the oven to 375°F (190°C).

2 Add the olive oil to an 8 in (20 cm) ovenproof, nonstick skillet set over low-medium heat. Once hot, add the onion and red pepper, and cook for 5 minutes until softened.

3 Meanwhile, crack the eggs into a bowl, season with salt and freshly ground black pepper, then whisk well and set aside.

4 Add the spinach and peas into the skillet, cook until the spinach has just wilted, then add the eggs. Tilt the pan so the base is evenly covered with the eggs, then sprinkle over the cheese.

5 Cook in the oven for 20 minutes, until it feels firm to touch.

6 Remove from the oven, slide out onto a plate, cut into squares or slices, and serve with toast, if you like.

Keep it This can be sliced up and stored in the fridge for up to 3 days.

Red peppers are a fabulous source of vitamin C. Weight for weight, they contain over twice as much vitamin C as oranges.

Whole Grain Bread

Kcals 190
Protein 53g
Fiber 6g

Makes 10 slices

Prep + cook time: 1 hour, plus proving

- 2⅓ cups (300g) whole wheat flour
- 1½ cups (200g) rye flour
- 2¼ tsp (7g) fast-action dried yeast
- 1 tbsp extra-virgin olive oil, plus extra for greasing
- 1 tsp molasses
- 1 tsp salt
- 1¾ cups (400ml) warm water

1 To a large bowl, add both flours, the yeast, olive oil, molasses, salt, and warm water. Mix with a spoon into a shaggy ball, then tip out onto a clean surface and knead for 10 minutes until smooth.

2 Lightly oil a large bowl, then add the dough. Cover with plastic wrap or a clean kitchen towel, then leave in a warm place for 1 hour, or until doubled in size.

3 Meanwhile, line a 9 x 5in loaf pan with parchment paper, then set aside.

4 Tip the dough out onto a clean surface, and knead again for 2 minutes. Place into the loaf pan, then cover and let prove for 1 hour until risen.

5 Meanwhile, preheat the oven to 425°F (220°C).

6 Bake for 40 minutes until golden (when you tap the base, it should sound hollow). Turn out onto a wire rack and let cool before slicing.

Keep it Slice this bread and keep in the freezer for up to 3 months. This can be toasted straight from frozen.

Whole wheat flour contains twice as much fiber as white flour, as well as higher levels of B vitamins.

Fiber-filled Lunches

Eating a high-fiber lunch will keep you feeling fuller for longer and help to avoid the dreaded afternoon slumps. These recipes have been designed to be packed with fiber, without compromising on flavor or satisfaction.

Carrot Ribbon Salad

Kcals 354
Protein 7g
Fiber 10g

Serves 2

Prep time: 5 minutes

- 3 large carrots, peeled and very thinly sliced
- 2 tbsp soy sauce
- 1 tbsp sesame oil
- 1 tbsp rice wine vinegar
- 1 clove of garlic, crushed
- 2 green onions, thinly sliced
- 2 tbsp sesame seeds
- ¼ cup (30g) walnut halves, roughly chopped

1 Add the carrots to a bowl with the soy sauce, sesame oil, rice wine vinegar, garlic, green onions, and sesame seeds. Toss together, then top with the walnuts and serve.

Swap it This would work well with zucchini instead of carrot.

Tip Serve alongside chicken or fish to turn this into a dinner.

It might be a myth that carrots help you see in the dark, but they do contain beta-carotene, a phytochemical that helps keep your eyes healthy in other ways.

Creamed Corn

Kcals 339
Protein 8g
Fiber 9g

Serves 4

Prep + cook time: 25 minutes

- 1 tbsp (15g) unsalted butter
- 2 x 9oz (255g) cans of sweet corn, drained
- 2 green onions, finely chopped
- 1 x 15oz (425g) can of lima beans, drained and rinsed, divided
- 2 cups (500ml) vegetable stock, divided
- 2 tbsp crème fraîche
- grated zest and juice of 1 lemon
- salt and freshly ground black pepper
- crispy chili oil, to serve (optional)

Crisp topping:

- ¼ cup (70ml) vegetable oil
- 1 leek, trimmed and thinly sliced
- 3 shallots, thinly sliced
- 10 cloves of garlic, thinly sliced

1 Add the butter to a saucepan set over medium heat. Once melted, add the sweet corn and green onions, then cook for 5 minutes, until the sweet corn is golden.

2 Add half of the sweet corn mix to a blender, along with half of the lima beans and half of the vegetable stock. Blend until smooth, then return to the sweet corn pan. Add in the remaining lima beans and remaining stock. Mix well, lower the heat, and cook for 15 minutes, until creamy.

3 Meanwhile, to make the crisp topping, add the vegetable oil to a skillet set over low-medium heat. Add the leek and shallots, then cook for about 8 minutes until golden. Remove with a slotted spoon and drain on some paper towels. Add in the garlic and cook for 1 minute, until golden. Remove the garlic with a slotted spoon and drain on paper towels. Set the crisp topping aside.

4 Add the crème fraîche and lemon juice to the sweet corn, then season with salt and freshly ground black pepper. Mix well.

5 Serve in bowls, topped with the crisp topping and crispy chili oil, if using.

Serve it This works really well with some fresh bread for scooping.

Onions contain a phytochemical called quercetin, which is believed to reduce the risk of heart disease as well as certain types of cancer.

Loaded Sweet Potatoes

Kcals 417
Protein 10g
Fiber 17g

Serves 2

Prep + cook time: 45 minutes

- 2 sweet potatoes
- 1 x 15oz (425g) can black beans, drained and rinsed
- 2 tsp chipotle en adobo
- 1 tsp maple syrup
- 1 avocado
- 1 tbsp sour cream
- juice of 1 lime
- handful of cilantro, roughly chopped
- salt
- 1 green chile, thinly sliced

1 Preheat the oven to 375°F (190°C).

2 Prick the sweet potatoes several times with a fork. Put onto a baking sheet and bake for 40 minutes until soft. Set aside.

3 Meanwhile, add the black beans and chipotle en adobo to a saucepan set over low heat, and cook for 3 minutes until the beans are warm. Add the maple syrup, mix well, then set aside.

4 In a small bowl, mash the avocado with a fork. Add sour cream, lime juice, and cilantro. Season with some salt, then mix and set aside.

5 Slice the potatoes in half lengthwise, then top with the black beans and avocado mixture. Finish by adding green chile slices.

Swap it The toppings on this sweet potato are easily adaptable—lima beans or chickpeas would work well in place of the black beans.

Avocados earn their superfood status thanks to the healthy fats they provide, as well as more than 20 different vitamins, minerals, and phytochemicals.

Lemony Butternut Squash and Quinoa Salad

Kcals 786
Protein 21g
Fiber 10g

Serves 2

Prep + cook time: 35 minutes

½ butternut squash, peeled and cut into 1¼ in (3 cm) chunks
2 tbsp extra-virgin olive oil
salt and freshly ground black pepper
1 x 9oz (250g) pouch of microwaveable quinoa
large handful of salad leaves
2 tbsp pumpkin seeds

Dressing:

3½oz (100g) feta
handful of cilantro
handful of flat-leaf parsley
grated zest and juice of 1 lemon
¼ cup (50ml) extra-virgin olive oil

Quinoa is a good source of protein and, unlike other grains, it contains all the essential amino acids.

1 Preheat the oven to 400°F (200°C).

2 Arrange the butternut squash on a large baking sheet in a single layer. Drizzle over the olive oil, then season with salt and freshly ground black pepper. Roast in the oven for 20 minutes until the butternut squash is tender. Set aside to cool.

3 Meanwhile, microwave the quinoa pouch according to the package instructions, then set aside to cool.

4 Spread the pumpkin seeds out on a small baking sheet, then cook in the oven for 5 minutes until the seeds smell lightly toasted.

5 Meanwhile, put all of the dressing ingredients into a blender and season with salt and freshly ground black pepper. Blend until smooth, adding a little water as needed if the dressing is too thick.

6 Add the salad leaves to a bowl along with the butternut squash and quinoa. Drizzle over the dressing and toss together. Sprinkle over the seeds and serve.

Keep it This butternut squash salad is great for prepping ahead—simply keep the salad leaves and dressing separate until ready to assemble. It will also keep for up to 2 days in the fridge.

Swap it To make this vegan, simply replace the feta with the same quantity of silken tofu.

Chicken Satay Salad

Kcals 486
Protein 47g
Fiber 7.5g

Serves 4

Prep + cook time:
25 minutes, plus marinating time

- ⅓ cup (70g) smooth peanut butter
- 1 tbsp fish sauce
- 1 tbsp soy sauce
- 2 cloves of garlic, crushed
- ¾ in (2 cm) piece of ginger, peeled and finely chopped
- 1 tbsp curry powder
- 1 tbsp maple syrup
- 4 chicken breasts
- 1 cup (200ml) coconut milk
- juice of 1 lime
- 2 tbsp vegetable oil, divided
- 3½oz (100g) broccolini
- 3½oz (100g) kale, stalks removed
- 2 carrots, peeled and cut into matchsticks
- 2 Boston lettuces, cut into wedges
- 3 tbsp pomegranate seeds
- ⅓ cup (50g) peanuts, roughly chopped

Broccoli is rich in vitamins B, C, and K.

1 To a small bowl add the peanut butter, fish sauce, soy sauce, garlic, ginger, curry powder, and maple syrup. Add a splash of water and whisk together.

2 Add the chicken to a large bowl, and pour over one-quarter of the sauce. Cover and marinate in the fridge for an hour, or overnight.

3 Meanwhile, pour the rest of the sauce into a saucepan. Add the coconut milk and lime juice, and bring to a gentle simmer. Cook for about 5 minutes until slightly thickened, then remove from the heat and set aside.

4 Add 1 tablespoon oil to a skillet set over high heat. Once hot, add the broccolini, then cook for 3 minutes on each side until charred and tender. Remove from the pan and set aside. Add the kale to the skillet and cook until just wilted, then remove from the pan and set aside with the broccolini.

5 Keep the skillet on the heat, and add the remaining tablespoon of oil to the pan. Add the chicken breasts to the pan and cook for about 5 minutes on each side until cooked through and golden. Remove from the heat and set aside.

6 To a platter, add the carrots, lettuce, broccolini, and kale. Slice the chicken and add to the platter. Drizzle over the sauce, then sprinkle over the pomegranate seeds and peanuts.

Swap it To make this vegetarian, swap the chicken for tofu and omit the fish sauce.

Lentil Flatbreads

Kcals 380
Protein 16g
Fiber 8g

Makes 4

Prep + cook time:
15 minutes, plus soaking and overnight resting

- 1 cup (200g) dried red lentils
- 1¾ cups (400ml)
- 1 tsp salt
- 2 zucchini, sliced
- 2 red onions, cut into small wedges
- 2 red peppers
- 1 tbsp dried oregano
- 2 tbsp vegetable oil, divided
- salt and freshly ground black pepper
- 2 lemons, halved
- 1 tbsp extra-virgin olive oil
- ⅓ cup (100g) hummus
- handful of basil
- handful of flat-leaf parsley

1 Add the red lentils to a bowl, cover with water, and let soak for 2–3 hours.

2 Drain the lentils, then add to a high-speed blender with 1¾ cups (400ml) water. Blend until smooth. Transfer this back into the bowl, then stir in the salt. Cover and leave in the fridge overnight.

3 To a bowl, add the zucchini, red onions, peppers, and oregano. Drizzle over 1 tablespoon vegetable oil, then season with salt and freshly ground black pepper. Mix well.

4 Set a griddle or skillet over high heat, then add in the vegetables. Cook for 3 minutes until charred and softened. Add them back into the bowl. When cool enough to handle, peel off and discard the skin from the peppers, then roughly chop and add back into the bowl.

5 Add the lemon to the griddle pan, cut-side down, and cook for 3 minutes until deeply charred and golden. Carefully squeeze the juice into the bowl of vegetables, then drizzle in the olive oil. Mix and set aside.

6 Add the remaining tablespoon of vegetable oil to a nonstick skillet set over medium heat. Add one-quarter of the batter, then spread around the pan using the back of the ladle. Cook for 2 minutes on each side. Remove from the pan and repeat to make four flatbreads.

7 Spread over the hummus, top with the griddled vegetables, basil, and parsley, and serve.

Lentils are particularly rich in soluble fiber, which forms a gel in the gut, helping to slow the absorption of sugar and reduce cholesterol levels.

Artichoke and Green Bean Salad

Kcals 625
Protein 19g
Fiber 14g

Serves 2

Prep + cook time: 20 minutes

- ¼ cup (50ml) extra-virgin olive oil
- 1 tbsp red wine vinegar
- handful of flat-leaf parsley, finely chopped
- handful of basil, finely chopped
- handful of mint, finely chopped
- grated zest and juice of 1 lemon
- 3 cloves of garlic, crushed, divided
- salt and freshly ground black pepper
- 1 x 15.5oz (439g) can of lima beans, drained and rinsed
- 7oz (200g) green beans, trimmed
- ⅓ cup (100g) Greek yogurt
- 3½oz (100g) artichoke hearts, drained

Dukkah:

- ¾ cup (100g) blanched almonds
- ¾ cup (100g) hazelnuts
- 1 tbsp cumin seeds
- 1 tbsp coriander seeds
- 1 tbsp fennel seeds
- 1 tbsp sesame seeds
- 1 tbsp nigella seeds

1 Preheat the oven to 400°F (200°C).

2 Put all of the dukkah ingredients onto a baking sheet and bake for 8 minutes until the nuts are golden. Transfer to a blender, along with a pinch of salt, and pulse until ground into a coarse blend, then set aside.

3 To a large bowl, add the olive oil, red wine vinegar, parsley, basil, mint, lemon zest, and 2 cloves of garlic. Season and whisk well. Stir in the lima beans, and let marinate.

4 Fill a saucepan with water and bring to a boil. Once boiling, add the green beans, then cook for 2 minutes until tender. Drain and set aside.

5 To a small bowl, add the Greek yogurt, the remaining clove of garlic, and the lemon juice. Season with salt and freshly ground black pepper, mix well, then spread out onto a platter. Top with the lima beans, green beans, and artichoke hearts. Sprinkle over some of the dukkah and serve.

Keep it Remaining dukkah can be stored in an airtight container for up to 2 weeks.

Artichoke hearts are rich in inulin, a type of prebiotic fibre.

Coronation Chicken and Chickpea Sandwich

Kcals 766
Protein 59g
Fiber 12g

Serves 4

Prep time: 15 minutes

- ½ red onion, thinly sliced
- juice of 1 lemon
- salt and freshly ground black pepper
- 1 cooked rotisserie chicken, meat shredded
- ⅓ cup (50g) almonds, roughly chopped
- ¼ cup (30g) dried apricots, roughly chopped
- 2½ tbsp (20g) raisins
- 3 tbsp mango chutney, divided
- ¼ cup (50g) Greek yogurt
- 2 tbsp mayonnaise
- 2 tsp curry powder
- 1 x 15oz (425g) can of chickpeas, drained and rinsed
- handful of cilantro, roughly chopped
- 8 slices of whole grain bread
- 2 large tomatoes, sliced
- ¼ cucumber, sliced
- handful of spinach

1 Add the red onion to a small bowl, squeeze in the lemon juice, and add a pinch of salt. Scrunch together with your hands, then set aside to pickle.

2 To a large bowl, add the shredded chicken, almonds, apricots, raisins, 1 tablespoon mango chutney, the Greek yogurt, mayonnaise, curry powder, chickpeas, and cilantro. Season with salt and freshly ground black pepper, then mix well and set aside.

3 Spread the remaining mango chutney over four slices of the bread, then top with slices of tomato and cucumber, spinach, the chicken filling, and pickled onions. Top with the remaining slices of bread and serve.

Keep it The coronation chicken filling will keep in the fridge for up to 4 days.

Chicken is an excellent source of protein and provides B vitamins, particularly thiamine and niacin.

Sardine Pasta

Kcals 632
Protein 26g
Fiber 14g

Serves 3

Prep + cook time: 20 minutes

- 2 tbsp extra-virgin olive oil
- 2 shallots, finely chopped
- 1 zucchini, thinly sliced
- 1 bulb of fennel, thinly sliced
- 7oz (200g) whole wheat spaghetti
- 3 cloves of garlic, thinly sliced
- pinch of chili flakes
- 3 tbsp capers
- ½ cup (70g) raisins
- ⅓ cup (50g) walnut halves, roughly chopped
- juice of 2 lemons
- 5oz (140g) can of sardines, drained, cut into 1¼ in (3 cm) pieces
- large handful of flat-leaf parsley, roughly chopped
- handful of dill, roughly chopped
- salt and freshly ground black pepper

1 Fill a large saucepan with water, season with salt, and bring to a boil.

2 Add the olive oil to a skillet set over low-medium heat. Add the shallots, zucchini, and fennel, then cook for 10 minutes until softened.

3 Meanwhile, add the pasta to the boiling water, then cook according to package instructions.

4 Add the garlic to the skillet, and cook for a further minute until fragrant.

5 Add in the chili flakes, capers, raisins, walnuts, lemon juice, sardines, and most of the parsley and dill. Season with salt and freshly ground black pepper.

6 Reserve a cup of pasta water. Drain the pasta, then add it to the skillet. Add a little of the pasta water and mix well until you have an emulsified sauce, then serve topped with the remaining herbs.

Keep it This will keep in the fridge for up to 3 days.

Canned sardines are a good source of omega-3 fats, calcium, and vitamin D, a nutrient which is often lacking in the diet.

Tofu Poke Bowl

Kcals 789
Protein 38g
Fiber 11g

Serves 2

Prep + cook time: 20 minutes

- 10½oz (300g) firm tofu, cut into 1¼in (3cm) cubes
- 1 tbsp cornstarch
- 2 tbsp vegetable oil
- 2 tbsp soy sauce
- 1 tbsp sriracha
- 1 tsp maple syrup or honey
- juice of 1 lime, divided
- 2 cloves of garlic
- ¾in (2cm) piece of ginger, peeled and finely chopped
- 1 x 9oz (250g) pouch of microwaveable brown basmati rice
- 3½oz (100g) radishes, thinly sliced
- 1 avocado, thinly sliced
- 3 tbsp kimchi
- ¾ cup (100g) edamame
- sesame seeds, to garnish

1 Pat the tofu dry with paper towels, sprinkle over the cornstarch, and toss so that all of the pieces are coated.

2 Add the vegetable oil to a skillet set over medium-high heat. Once hot, add the tofu and fry for about 10 minutes, turning the pieces around until golden in color.

3 Meanwhile, to a small bowl, add the soy sauce, sriracha, maple syrup or honey, half of the lime juice, the garlic, and ginger. Mix well, then add to the skillet and cook for 1 minute. Remove from the heat and set aside.

4 Microwave the rice pouch according to the package instructions, then divide between two bowls. Top with the tofu, radishes, avocado, kimchi, and edamame. Squeeze over the remaining lime juice, garnish with sesame seeds, and serve.

Swap it Chicken or salmon would also work.

Edamame beans are rich in vitamins A, C, and K, and soluble fiber. They are a useful source of iron and protein, too.

Beet and Lentil Salad

Kcals 758
Protein 34g
Fiber 14.5g

Serves 2

Prep + cook time: 45 minutes

- 1 cup (200g) dried green lentils
- 4 cups (1 liter) water
- 4 cloves of garlic, 2 peeled and lightly bashed, 2 crushed
- 3 sprigs of thyme
- 2 sprigs of rosemary
- salt and freshly ground black pepper
- 1 tbsp red wine vinegar
- 1 tsp Dijon mustard
- 1 tsp maple syrup
- 3 tbsp extra-virgin olive oil
- 1 tsp dried oregano
- 2 cooked beets, cut into 1¼ in (3 cm) chunks
- ⅓ cup (50g) walnut halves, chopped
- 1¾oz (50g) feta
- chopped flat-leaf parsley, to serve

1 Add the green lentils to a sieve and rinse under cold water, then add to a large saucepan and cover with the water.

2 Add the 2 garlic cloves and the thyme and rosemary sprigs. Bring to a boil and cook for 10 minutes.

3 Reduce the heat, cover, and cook for 30 minutes until the lentils are tender. Drain any water that remains. Season with salt and freshly ground black pepper, remove the herb sprigs and garlic cloves, and set aside.

4 To a large bowl, add the red wine vinegar, Dijon mustard, maple syrup, olive oil and oregano. Season with salt and freshly ground black pepper, then whisk well. Add the lentils to the bowl and mix well.

5 Arrange the lentil salad on a platter, top with the beet and walnuts, crumble over the feta, and serve with a sprinkle of chopped parsley.

Keep it This will keep in the fridge for up to 3 days.

Beets contain phytochemicals called nitrates, which relax and dilate blood vessels, helping to reduce high blood pressure and improve the flow of blood to the brain.

Beef Kofta Grain Bowl

Kcals 718
Protein 43g
Fiber 13g

Serves 4

Prep + cook time: 40 minutes

- 2⅓ cups (400g) bulgur wheat
- 3¼ cups (800ml) water
- salt and freshly ground black pepper
- 1lb 2oz (500g) 5% fat ground beef
- 1 zucchini, grated
- 1 red onion, half grated, half thinly sliced
- large bunch of flat-leaf parsley, chopped
- 2 cloves of garlic, crushed
- ¾in (2 cm) piece of ginger, peeled and finely chopped
- grated zest and juice of 1 lemon
- 1 tbsp ground cumin
- 1 tsp paprika
- 2 tsp allspice
- 1 tsp ground coriander
- 7oz (200g) green beans, trimmed
- 2 tbsp extra-virgin olive oil
- 3½oz (100g) pomegranate seeds
- handful of baby spinach

Tahini yogurt:

- 3 tbsp Greek yogurt
- 2 tbsp tahini
- 1 tsp maple syrup

1 Add the bulgur wheat to a sieve and rinse under cold water, then add to a saucepan. Top with the water, season with salt, then set over high heat and bring to a boil. Once boiling, turn the heat down to low, cover, and cook for 20 minutes until tender. Fluff up with a fork and set aside.

2 Meanwhile, add the ground beef, zucchini, grated red onion, a small handful of the chopped parsley (reserving the majority for the salad), garlic, ginger, lemon zest, cumin, paprika, allspice, and ground coriander to a bowl. Season with salt and pepper, then shape into 20 koftas. Set aside.

3 Cook the green beans in a pan of boiling water for 2 minutes until tender. Drain and set aside.

4 Add the olive oil to a large saucepan set over medium-high heat. Add the koftas and cook for about 10 minutes, occasionally turning them in the pan, until cooked through. Set aside.

5 To a small bowl, add the sliced red onion, remaining parsley, and pomegranate seeds. Add the lemon juice and season with salt. Set aside.

6 Add the yogurt, tahini, and maple syrup to a small bowl, and season with salt and freshly ground black pepper. Whisk well and add a little water if needed if mixture is too thick.

7 Divide the bulgur among bowls. Top with the koftas, green beans, baby spinach, and red onion salad. Drizzle over the tahini yogurt and serve.

Kale and Chickpea Caesar Salad

Kcals	641
Protein	19g
Fiber	14g

Serves 2

Prep + cook time: 40 minutes

- 14oz (400g) kale
- 3 tbsp extra-virgin olive oil, divided
- juice of 1 lemon
- salt
- ½ red onion, thinly sliced
- 3 slices of whole wheat bread
- 1 x 15oz (425g) can of chickpeas, drained and rinsed
- 3½oz (100g) sun-dried tomatoes, chopped
- 2 avocados, chopped

Dressing:

- ⅔ cup (140g) crème fraîche
- ¼ cup (50g) Greek yogurt
- 2 tsp Dijon mustard
- 4 anchovy fillets
- 2 tsp white wine vinegar
- 1 clove of garlic
- 3 tbsp grated Parmesan cheese, plus extra to serve

Kale is an excellent source of vitamin K, which is important for healthy bones.

1 Preheat the oven to 400°F (200°C).

2 Remove the stalks from the kale, shred the leaves, and add to a large bowl. Add 1 tablespoon olive oil, half the lemon juice, and a pinch of salt. Scrunch together with your hands for a minute, then set aside to soften.

3 To a small bowl, add the red onion, remaining lemon juice, and a pinch of salt. Scrunch together with your hands and set aside to pickle.

4 Cut the bread into 3cm (1¼in) chunks and arrange on a baking sheet. Pour over 1 tablespoon olive oil and season with a pinch of salt. Cook for 10 minutes until golden and crispy.

5 Meanwhile, arrange the chickpeas on a separate baking sheet and pat dry with paper towels. Pour over the remaining 1 tablespoon olive oil and cook for 15–20 minutes until crispy, then set aside.

6 Add the croutons to a blender and blend until you have bread crumbs, then set aside.

7 To the same blender, add all the dressing ingredients and blend until smooth.

8 Pour the dressing into the kale bowl. Add in the crispy chickpeas, sun-dried tomatoes, and avocados. Toss together, then top with the pickled onions, bread crumbs, and Parmesan cheese.

Tip Add in some rotisserie chicken to make this a summer dinner.

Midweek Dinners

These fiber-rich midweek dinners are quick and easy to prepare when time is short. From steak tacos to pasta and ramen, there is something here to satisfy any craving after a busy day.

Kimchi Stir-Fry

Kcals	432
Protein	15g
Fiber	8g

Serves 4

Prep + cook time: 15 minutes

- 1 tbsp vegetable oil
- 1 head of broccoli, cut into florets
- 1 red pepper, seeded and cut into ½in (1cm) chunks
- ¾ cup (100g) cashews
- 7oz (200g) kimchi, plus 1 tbsp kimchi liquid
- ¾ cup (100g) frozen peas
- 3 cloves of garlic, crushed
- ¾in (2cm) piece of ginger, peeled and finely chopped
- 1 tbsp gochujang
- 2 tbsp soy sauce
- 1 tsp sesame oil
- ⅓ cup (100ml) water
- 2 x 9oz (250g) pouches of microwaveable brown basmati rice
- juice of 1 lime,plus extra lime slices to serve (optional)
- 2 green onions, thinly sliced

1 Add the vegetable oil to a wok or large skillet set over high heat. Once hot, add the broccoli, red pepper, cashews, kimchi, and peas. Cook for 1 minute, continuously moving everything around in the pan.

2 Add in the garlic and ginger, and cook for 10 seconds. Add in the gochujang, soy sauce, sesame oil, kimchi liquid, and water.

3 Cook the rice according to the package instructions, then add it to the skillet, breaking it apart with a wooden spoon and cook for a further minute until piping hot.

4 Squeeze over the lime juice, sprinkle over the green onions, and serve with extra lime slices, if liked.

Tip Chicken or steak could also be added to this dish.

Fermented foods like kimchi are rich in probiotic friendly bacteria, which help keep your gut healthy.

Crispy Tofu Noodles

Kcals 799
Protein 39g
Fiber 10g

Serves 2

Prep + cook time: 20 minutes

- 2 tbsp vegetable oil
- 7oz (200g) firm tofu, patted dry and grated
- 1 tsp five spice powder
- 2 tbsp soy sauce
- 1 tbsp hoisin sauce
- 7oz (200g) buckwheat noodles
- 3½oz (100g) green beans, trimmed and halved
- 3½oz (100g) bok choy, leaves separated

Sauce:

- 2 tbsp soy sauce
- 2 tbsp tahini
- 1 clove of garlic, crushed
- ¾in (2cm) piece of ginger, peeled and finely chopped
- 1 tsp ground Sichuan pepper (optional)
- 2 tsp crispy chili oil, plus extra to serve
- 2 tbsp warm water

1 Add the vegetable oil to a skillet set over medium-high heat. Once hot, add the tofu and cook for 10 minutes until crispy. Add in the five spice powder, soy sauce, and hoisin sauce, and cook for a further 30 seconds, then remove from the heat and set aside.

2 Meanwhile, add all the ingredients for the sauce to a small bowl. Mix well and divide the sauce between two bowls.

3 Fill a large saucepan with water and bring to a boil. Add the noodles and cook according to package instructions, adding in the green beans and bok choy 1 minute before the end of cooking time. Drain, then divide the noodles and vegetables between the serving bowls.

4 Top with the crispy tofu and a little extra crispy chili oil, then mix everything together and serve.

Swap it You can swap the tofu for ground pork.

Tofu is packed with protein, selenium, calcium, copper, and phosphorus, as well as phytochemicals, which help reduce cholesterol levels.

Broccoli Pesto Pasta

Kcals 671
Protein 26g
Fiber 18g

Serves 4

Prep + cook time: 20 minutes

- ½ cup (70g) walnut halves
- 1 head of broccoli, cut into florets, stalks sliced
- 1¾oz (50g) basil
- 2½oz (75g) arugula
- 1 clove of garlic, crushed
- ⅓ cup (30g) finely grated Parmesan cheese, plus extra to serve
- grated zest and juice of 1 lemon
- salt and freshly ground black pepper
- 3½ tbsp (50ml) extra-virgin olive oil
- 12oz (350g) whole wheat pasta
- 1 x 15oz (425g) can of chickpeas, drained and rinsed

1 Add the walnuts to a small saucepan set over medium heat. Cook for about 4 minutes until the walnuts are toasted, then set aside.

2 Fill a large saucepan with water, salt the water, and bring to a boil. Once boiling, add the broccoli and cook for 1 minute until slightly softened. Scoop the broccoli out with a slotted spoon and transfer to a blender. Keep the water boiling for the pasta.

3 To the blender, add the walnuts, basil, arugula, garlic, Parmesan cheese, lemon zest and juice, and olive oil. Season with salt and freshly ground black pepper and pulse until combined but not totally smooth, then set aside.

4 Add the pasta to the pan of boiling water, then cook according to package instructions. Reserve a cup of the pasta water, then drain.

5 Add the pasta back into the pan. Add in the pesto, a little of the reserved pasta water, and the chickpeas. Mix until the sauce looks creamy, and serve with a little extra Parmesan cheese.

Swap it The walnuts can be swapped for pistachios or pine nuts.

Using walnuts instead of pine nuts to make the pesto helps boost the omega-3 content of this dish, and adds vitamin E, B1, iron, and zinc.

Cauliflower Steaks with Herby Sauce

Kcals 390
Protein 12g
Fiber 10g

Serves 2

Prep + cook time: 25 minutes

- ½ large head of cauliflower, cut into 1¼in- (3 cm-) thick steaks
- 4 tbsp extra-virgin olive oil, divided
- salt and freshly ground black pepper
- 1 tsp Dijon mustard
- handful of flat-leaf parsley, finely chopped
- 1 tbsp capers, roughly chopped
- ½ red onion, finely chopped
- juice of ½ lemon
- 1 x 9oz (250g) pouch of microwaveable puy lentils

1 Preheat the oven to 425°F (220°C).

2 Arrange the cauliflower on a large baking sheet in a single layer. Drizzle over 2 tablespoons olive oil, then season with salt and freshly ground black pepper. Roast in the oven for 15–20 minutes until the cauliflower is tender.

3 Meanwhile, to a small bowl, add the Dijon mustard, parsley, capers, red onion, lemon juice, and remaining 2 tablespoons olive oil. Season with salt and freshly ground black pepper, mix well, and set aside.

4 Microwave the puy lentils for 2 minutes.

5 Divide the lentils and cauliflower steaks between two plates and spoon over the dressing.

Keep it This impressive vegan dish can be prepared well ahead of time. Keep the salsa verde in the fridge until ready to serve, then all you have to do is cook the cauliflower and you are good to go!

Cauliflower, like other cruciferous vegetables, is rich in nutrients that help lower blood pressure and regulate cholesterol.

Steak Tacos with Corn Salsa

Kcals 867
Protein 63g
Fiber 17g

Serves 4

Prep + cook time: 20 minutes

- 1 tbsp (15g) unsalted butter
- 1½ cups (200g) frozen corn
- ½ red onion
- large handful of cilantro, chopped
- 2 large tomatoes, seeded and chopped
- 1 green chile, seeded and finely chopped
- ⅔ cup (100g) canned black beans, drained and rinsed
- juice of 2 limes, divided, plus wedges to serve
- salt
- ¼ red cabbage, shredded
- 2 avocados
- 1 tbsp Greek yogurt
- 1 tbsp extra-virgin olive oil
- 2 thick sirloin steaks, about 1¾lb (800g) total weight
- 12 small whole wheat flour tortillas

1 Add the butter to a skillet set over high heat. Once hot, add the corn and cook for around 5 minutes until golden in color. Transfer to a bowl.

2 To the corn, add the red onion, half of the cilantro, the tomatoes, green chile, black beans, and the juice of 1 lime. Season with salt, then mix well and set aside.

3 Add the red cabbage to a small bowl, then season with a little salt and set aside.

4 Add the avocados to a small bowl and mash with a fork. Add in the Greek yogurt, the remaining lime juice, and the remaining cilantro. Season with salt, then mix well and set aside.

5 Add the olive oil to a skillet set over high heat. Once hot, add the steaks to the pan and cook for 2 minutes on each side for medium rare. Remove from the pan and set aside to rest for 10 minutes.

6 Meanwhile, warm the tortillas in a pan or microwave.

7 Slice the steaks, then assemble the tacos: spread over some avocado mixture, then top with the steak, some cabbage, and some of the corn salsa. Serve with lime wedges.

Swap it Chicken or shrimp would also work well here.

The phytochemical anthocyanin (which gives red cabbage its color) is good for the heart and can help improve blood flow to the brain.

Shepherd's Pie

Kcals 782
Protein 42g
Fiber 19g

Serves 4

Prep + cook time: 1 hour 10 minutes

- 2 tbsp extra-virgin olive oil
- 1 onion, finely chopped
- 2 carrots, peeled and finely chopped
- 2 stalks of celery, finely chopped
- 3 cloves of garlic, crushed
- 1lb 2oz (500g) 10% fat ground lamb
- 2 tbsp harissa
- 2 bay leaves
- 2 cups (500ml) beef stock
- 1 x 15.5oz (439g) can of kidney beans, drained and rinsed
- salt and freshly ground black pepper
- 2lb (900g) sweet potatoes, peeled and cut into large chunks
- 3 tbsp (40g) unsalted butter
- 3 tbsp milk
- 1½ cups (200g) frozen peas

1 Add the oil to a large skillet set over medium heat. Add the onion, carrots, celery, and garlic, and cook for 10 minutes until softened.

2 Add in the ground lamb and cook for about 10 minutes until browned. Add in the harissa and cook for 30 seconds, then add the bay leaves, beef stock, and kidney beans. Season with salt and freshly ground black pepper, then reduce the heat to low and simmer for about 20 minutes, or until the liquid has slightly thickened.

3 Preheat the oven to 375°F (190°C).

4 Meanwhile, fill a large saucepan with water and bring to a boil. Once boiling, add the sweet potatoes and cook for 10–15 minutes, until tender. Drain, then mash with a potato masher and add in the butter and milk.

5 Put the lamb filling into a large ovenproof dish, and sprinkle over the peas. Top with the mash and smooth over with a spoon. Cook in the oven for 25 minutes until bubbling and golden.

Keep it This will keep in the fridge for up to 5 days.

Peas are a good source of soluble fiber, which can help reduce blood cholesterol levels. They also provide good amounts of vitamins A, C, and K.

Thai-style Salmon Fish Cakes

Kcals	431
Protein	31.5g
Fiber	5g

Serves 4

Prep + cook time: 25 minutes, plus soaking time

- ¼ cup (50g) dried red lentils
- 4 salmon fillets, skin removed
- 1 tbsp fish sauce
- 1 tbsp red curry paste
- small bunch of cilantro, roughly chopped
- 2 green onions, roughly chopped
- ¾ cup (100g) frozen peas or edamame
- 2 carrots, peeled, cut into matchsticks
- 5 radishes, sliced
- juice of 1 lime
- 2 tbsp soy sauce
- 2 tbsp vegetable oil

1 Add the red lentils to a bowl, cover them with cold water, and let soak for 2 hours.

2 Drain the lentils, then add them to a blender with the salmon fillets, fish sauce, red curry paste, cilantro, and green onions. Blend until the mixture comes together, then shape into four patties. Put them onto a baking sheet, then place in the fridge for 10 minutes to firm up.

3 Meanwhile, fill a small saucepan with water and bring to a boil. Once boiling, add the peas or edamame and cook for 30 seconds, then drain and add to a bowl. Add the carrots, radishes, lime juice, and soy sauce, then mix together. Set aside.

4 Add the oil to a saucepan and set over medium-high heat. Once hot, add the fish cakes and cook for 4 minutes on each side until cooked through. Serve alongside the salad.

Keep it These fish cakes can be frozen for up to 3 months.

Salmon contains omega-3 fats, which help reduce the risk of heart disease and stroke. We should aim to eat at least one portion of oil-rich fish, like salmon, a week.

Chicken with Leeks and Lima Beans

Kcals 570
Protein 62g
Fiber 15g

Serves 2

Prep + cook time: 50 minutes

- 1 tbsp extra-virgin olive oil
- 4 chicken thighs or legs
- 2 leeks, finely chopped
- 2 cloves of garlic, crushed
- 2 sprigs of thyme
- 1 tbsp miso paste
- 1 cup (200ml) chicken stock
- juice of 2 lemons
- 1 x 15oz (425g) can of lima beans
- ½ cup (50g) pitted green olives, halved
- 3½oz (100g) asparagus, trimmed and halved
- 7oz (200g) spinach, roughly chopped
- salt and freshly ground black pepper
- handful of flat-leaf parsley, roughly chopped
- handful of dill, roughly chopped

1 Add the olive oil to a high-sided skillet set over medium heat. Once hot, add the chicken, skin-side down, and cook for about 15 minutes until golden in color. The skin should release from the pan when it is ready. Remove from the pan, then set aside.

2 Add the leeks, garlic, and thyme to the pan, then cook for about 10 minutes until softened.

3 To a bowl, add the miso and chicken stock, then whisk and add into the pan.

4 Add the lemon juice, lima beans (along with the liquid from the can), olives, asparagus, spinach, and chicken to the pan, placing the chicken in the pan skin-side up.

5 Turn the heat down to low and let it simmer for 10–15 minutes until the chicken is cooked through.

6 Season, sprinkle over the herbs, and serve.

Tip This would be equally as delicious without the chicken to keep it vegetarian.

Asparagus and leeks contain fructo-oligosaccharides, a type of prebiotic fiber that encourages friendly gut bacteria.

Spring Green Pearl Barley Risotto

Kcals 922
Protein 29g
Fiber 11g

Serves 2

Prep + cook time: 50 minutes

- 10½oz (300g) Tuscan kale, stalks removed
- 1 clove of garlic, crushed
- juice of 1 lemon
- 1 tbsp extra-virgin olive oil
- 2 shallots, finely chopped
- 9oz (250g) pearl barley
- ⅔ cup (150ml) white wine
- 4 cups (1 liter) vegetable stock
- 5¼oz (150g) asparagus, finely chopped into rounds
- ¾ cup (100g) peas
- ⅔ cup (40g) grated Parmesan cheese
- 2 tbsp (30g) unsalted butter
- salt and freshly ground black pepper

1 Fill a large saucepan with water, then bring to a boil. Once boiling, add the Tuscan kale and cook for 1 minute. Reserve a cup of the cooking water, then drain the kale and transfer to a blender.

2 Add the garlic and lemon juice to the blender, along with a little of the cooking water, and blend until smooth, then set aside.

3 Add the olive oil to a high-sided skillet set over low-medium heat. Once hot, add the shallots, and cook for 5 minutes until softened. Add the pearl barley and cook for 3 minutes until it smells nutty.

4 Add in the white wine and cook until the liquid has been reduced by half.

5 Start adding the stock, a ladleful at a time, stirring continuously for about 25 minutes, until the barley is almost tender. Just after the final ladleful of stock, add in the asparagus, peas, and kale sauce. Stir through, then cook until the pearl barley is tender.

6 Add the Parmesan cheese and butter, season with salt and freshly ground black pepper, and serve.

Tip This would also work well with the addition of cod or salmon.

Barley contains beta-glucans, a type of soluble fiber, which helps reduce bad LDL blood cholesterol.

Pork and Miso Ramen

Kcals	706
Protein	47g
Fiber	8g

Serves 4

Prep + cook time: 35 minutes

- 2 tbsp vegetable oil
- 10½oz (300g) shiitake mushrooms, roughly chopped
- 14oz (400g) ground pork
- 3 cloves of garlic, crushed
- 1¼in (3cm) piece of ginger, peeled and finely chopped
- 3 green onions, finely chopped
- 1 tbsp chili garlic sauce or sriracha
- 2 tbsp white miso paste
- 2 tbsp soy sauce
- 3¼ cups (800ml) chicken stock
- 14oz (400g) buckwheat soba noodles
- 5¼oz (150g) bok choy, leaves separated
- 1½ cups (200g) frozen corn

1 Add the oil to a large saucepan set over medium-high heat. Once hot, add the mushrooms and ground pork and cook for 5 minutes, until both are browned. Add in the garlic, ginger, and green onions and cook for 1 minute until fragrant.

2 Add the chili sauce and miso paste. Cook for 30 seconds, then add the soy and chicken stock. Lower the heat and cook for about 15 minutes.

3 Meanwhile, fill a medium saucepan with water and bring to a boil. Add the noodles and cook according to the package instructions. Drain in a sieve, run under cold water, and set aside.

4 Add the bok choy to the broth and cook for 3 minutes until al dente. Add in the corn and cook for 30 seconds. Add the noodles to the broth to warm through, divide among bowls, and serve.

Swap it This would also work well with ground chicken.

Shiitake mushrooms contain phytochemicals, which are believed to reduce the risk of certain types of cancer.

Spinach and Chickpea Thai-style Curry

Kcals	625
Protein	17g
Fiber	12g

Serves 4

Prep + cook time: 20 minutes

- 1 tbsp vegetable or coconut oil
- 3 cloves of garlic, crushed
- ¾ in (2 cm) piece of ginger, peeled and finely chopped
- 2 tbsp Thai red curry paste
- 10½oz (300g) sweet potatoes, peeled and cut into 1¼ in (3 cm) chunks
- 2 x 15oz (425g) cans of chickpeas, drained and rinsed
- 1 x 13.5oz (400g) can of coconut milk
- 1¼ cups (300ml) vegetable stock
- 2 tbsp soy sauce
- 2 x 9oz (250g) pouches of microwaveable brown basmati rice
- 7oz (200g) spinach
- juice of 2 limes
- salt

1 Add the oil to a large saucepan set over low-medium heat. Once hot, add the garlic and ginger, and cook for 30 seconds until fragrant. Add the Thai red curry paste and cook for a further 30 seconds.

2 Add the sweet potatoes, chickpeas, coconut milk, vegetable stock, and soy sauce. Bring to a boil, then reduce to a low simmer. Cook for 15 minutes until the sweet potatoes are tender.

3 Meanwhile, microwave the rice pouches according to the package instructions.

4 Add the spinach to the curry and stir through until just wilted. Add the lime juice and season with salt.

5 Divide the curry among bowls and serve with the rice.

Keep it This can be frozen for up to 3 months.

Spinach is an excellent source of the B vitamin folate, which is essential for the production of red blood cells and the release of energy.

Batch Cooking & Meal Prep

On days where you're short on time, batch cooking is your secret weapon. Having something homemade and nutritious prepared can also help you keep track of your daily fiber intake, since you know exactly what is in it.

Cabbage Rolls

Kcals 474
Protein 15g
Fiber 12g

Serves 2

Prep + cook time:
1 hour 10 minutes

- 8 large savoy or Napa cabbage leaves
- 2 tbsp extra-virgin olive oil
- 1 onion, finely chopped
- 2 cloves of garlic, crushed
- 1 x 9oz (250g) pouch of microwaveable lentils
- 1 x 9oz (250g) pouch of microwaveable brown basmati rice
- 1½oz (40g) dried apricots, finely chopped
- ¾ cup (20g) finely chopped parsley
- ⅓ cup (15g) finely chopped cilantro
- juice of 1 lemon
- ⅔ cup (150ml) passata
- salt and freshly ground black pepper

1 Preheat the oven to 375°F (190°C).

2 Fill a large saucepan with water and bring to a boil. Add the cabbage leaves and cook for 5 minutes, until softened. Drain and run under cold water, then set aside.

3 Add the olive oil to a skillet set over low–medium heat. Once hot, add the onion and garlic, then cook for 10 minutes, until softened. Add the pouch of lentils, pouch of rice, dried apricots, parsley, cilantro, lemon juice, and half of the passata. Season with salt and black pepper, and cook for a further 5 minutes until softened.

4 Lay the cabbage leaves out flat and remove the stalk from each leaf. Put a couple of tablespoons of the mixture into the center of each leaf. Fold the sides in, then roll the leaf away from you, making sure no edges are exposed.

5 Put the cabbage rolls into a baking dish, making sure that the cabbage rolls fit snuggly. Pour the remaining passata around the cabbage rolls. Cover tightly with aluminum foil, and cook for 40 minutes, until softened.

Serve it These cabbage rolls can be enjoyed on their own or alongside some whole wheat bread.

Savoy cabbage is a great source of vitamin C, which aids the absorption of energizing iron found in the lentils.

Tomato and Chickpea Curry

Kcals 243
Protein 12g
Fiber 12g

Serves 2

Prep + cook time: 25 minutes

- 1 tbsp extra-virgin olive oil
- ½ onion, finely chopped
- 2 cloves of garlic, crushed
- ½ in (1cm) piece of ginger, finely chopped
- 1 tbsp Madras curry powder
- ¼ tsp ground turmeric
- 1 x 14oz (411g) can diced tomatoes
- 1 large tomato, grated
- 1 x 15oz (425g) can chickpeas, drained and rinsed
- juice of 1 lime
- salt

To serve (optional):

- naan
- chopped cilantro
- raita

1 Add the olive oil to a high-sided skillet set over low-medium heat. Once hot, add the onion, garlic, and ginger. Cook for 5 minutes, until softened. Add the curry powder and turmeric, and cook for 30 seconds, until fragrant.

2 Add the diced tomatoes, grated tomato, and chickpeas, then cover and cook for about 15 minutes, until the sauce has slightly reduced.

3 Add the lime juice, and season with salt.

4 Serve with naan, cilantro, and some raita, if liked.

Tip This curry is a great staple when you are short on time, without compromising on flavor, comfort, and nourishment.

As well as providing more fiber, chickpeas are a great plant-based protein source.

Sweet Potato Soup

Kcals 484
Protein 6g
Fiber 11g

Serves 4

Prep + cook time:
45 minutes

- 1lb 9oz (700g) sweet potatoes, peeled and roughly chopped
- 1 carrot, roughly chopped
- 2 red peppers, seeded and roughly chopped
- 1 onion, roughly chopped
- 1 bulb of garlic, halved horizontally
- 1 tbsp ground cumin
- 1 tbsp smoked paprika
- 1 tsp chipotle flakes
- 1 tbsp dried oregano
- salt and freshly ground black pepper
- 3 tbsp extra-virgin olive oil
- 2½ cups (600ml) vegetable or chicken stock
- 1 x 13.5oz (400ml) can of coconut milk
- juice of 1 lime

To serve (optional):

- Dukkah (see p59)
- chopped chives

1 Preheat the oven to 375°F (190°C).

2 To a large baking sheet, add the sweet potatoes, carrot, red peppers, onion, garlic, cumin, paprika, chipotle flakes, and oregano. Season with salt and freshly ground black pepper, then drizzle over the olive oil. Cook for 35 minutes, until vegetables are tender.

3 Squeeze the garlic out of its skin, then transfer the mix to a large saucepan. Add the stock, coconut milk, and lime juice. Season with salt and freshly ground black pepper, then blend with an immersion blender until smooth. Place over high heat and bring to a boil.

4 Serve in bowls, topped with the dukkah and chopped chives, if using.

Swap it The sweet potatoes can be swapped for butternut squash.

Sweet potatoes are rich in vitamins A and C, along with the minerals manganese and potassium.

Sausage and Mushroom Ragù

Kcals 557
Protein 27g
Fiber 11.5g

Serves 4

Prep + cook time:
40 minutes

- 1oz (30g) dried porcini mushrooms
- 1 cup (200ml) boiling water
- 2 tbsp extra-virgin olive oil
- 6 pork sausages
- 2 cloves of garlic, crushed
- 9oz (250g) brown button mushrooms, finely chopped
- 2 bay leaves
- 1 cup (150g) canned green lentils, drained
- 1 cup (200g) canned black beans, drained
- 1 tbsp miso paste
- 1 tbsp soy sauce
- 1 tbsp harissa
- 1 tbsp tomato paste
- 2 x 14oz (411g) cans of roma tomatoes
- salt and freshly ground black pepper
- ½ cup (40g) finely grated Parmesan cheese
- large handful of flat-leaf parsley, roughly chopped

1 Put the porcini mushrooms in a bowl and pour the boiling water over them, then set aside.

2 Add the olive oil to a large skillet set over medium-high heat. Once hot, squeeze the sausagemeat out of their skins into the pan and cook for 5 minutes, until golden.

3 Add in the garlic and brown button mushrooms, then cook for 5 minutes, until golden, breaking up the sausagemeat with a wooden spoon.

4 Add the bay leaves, lentils, black beans, miso paste, soy, harissa, tomato paste, and roma tomatoes. Break the tomatoes up with a wooden spoon, then season with salt and pepper. Lower the heat, cover, and let the ragù simmer for 20 minutes until reduced.

5 Stir in the Parmesan cheese and parsley and serve.

Keep it This can be frozen for up to 3 months.

Mushrooms contain the phytochemicals chitin and lentinan, which could help strengthen the immune system and reduce blood pressure.

Butternut Squash Gnocchi

Kcals 797
Protein 27g
Fiber 15.5g

Serves 2

Prep + cook time: 40 minutes

- 1lb 2oz (500g) butternut squash, peeled and cut into rough chunks
- 1 cup (120g) 00 flour or all-purpose flour, plus extra for dusting
- 9oz (250g) broccolini
- 2 tbsp (30g) unsalted butter
- ½ cup (70g) hazelnuts
- handful of sage, leaves picked
- 3½oz (100g) spinach
- juice of 1 lemon
- 2 tbsp grated Parmesan cheese
- salt and freshly ground black pepper

Butternut squash is a great source of beta-carotene, which helps keep skin healthy and improves skin tone and appearance.

1 Preheat the oven to 400°F (200°C).

2 Put the butternut squash onto a baking sheet and cook for 20 minutes, until tender. Transfer to a blender and blend until smooth, then let cool.

3 Add the flour to a bowl, then add in the cooled butternut squash purée and knead for 1 minute until you have a smooth dough.

4 Sprinkle a little extra flour onto a large baking sheet, then divide the dough in two. Roll each portion of dough into a log about 1¾in (4 cm) in diameter. With a sharp knife, or dough scraper, cut the logs into 1¾in (4 cm) pieces. Put the pieces onto the floured baking sheet. Set aside.

5 Cook the broccolini in a pan of salted boiling water for about a minute until tender. Remove with a slotted spoon and set aside.

6 Add the butter to a large skillet set over medium heat. Add the hazelnuts and cook until they smell nutty.

7 Add the gnocchi to the boiling water and cook for 1–2 minutes until they float to the surface. Using a slotted spoon, transfer the gnocchi into the skillet. Stir in the broccolini, sage, spinach, and lemon juice. Cook until the spinach is wilted.

8 Sprinkle over the Parmesan cheese and serve.

Keep it Once the gnocchi is boiled, it can be kept on an oiled baking sheet in the fridge for 3 days.

Nutty Oat Bread

Kcals 302
Protein 10.5g
Fiber 4.5g

Makes 10 slices

Prep + cook time: 40 minutes

- 1 cup (250g) plain yogurt
- 5 cups (500g) old-fashioned rolled oats
- ½ cup (80g) mixed nuts (such as almonds, walnut halves, cashews, and macadamia nuts)
- ¼ cup (30g) golden raisins
- ½ tsp baking soda
- 1 tsp salt
- 2 eggs
- 3 tbsp milk

1 Preheat the oven to 400°F (200°C). Line a 9 x 5 in loaf pan with parchment paper, then set aside.

2 To a large bowl, add the yogurt, oats, nuts, golden raisins, baking soda, salt, eggs, and milk. Mix well.

3 Add the mixture to the loaf pan and smooth out with a spoon. With a sharp knife, score a light line down the middle, vertically.

4 Cook for 30 minutes, until golden.

5 Remove from the oven, then let cool completely in the pan.

Keep it This loaf can be sliced up and stored in the freezer for up to 1 month.

Oats are an excellent source of soluble fiber, which can help reduce blood cholesterol levels. Adding nuts helps boost the protein and adds healthy fats.

Chickpea and Fennel Soup

Kcals 392
Protein 16g
Fiber 13.5g

Serves 4

Prep + cook time:
25 minutes

- 2 tbsp extra-virgin olive oil
- 1 bulb of fennel, sliced
- 1 tsp fennel seeds
- 1 onion, sliced
- 3 cloves of garlic, crushed
- 1 leek, sliced
- 3 sprigs of thyme
- 1 tbsp rosemary, roughly chopped
- salt and freshly ground black pepper
- ¾ cup (100g) walnut halves
- 2 x 15oz (425g) cans of chickpeas, drained and rinsed
- 3 cups (700ml) vegetable stock
- juice of 2 lemons
- handful of dill, roughly chopped
- pinch of chili flakes

1 Add the olive oil to a large saucepan set over low-medium heat. Once hot, add the fennel, fennel seeds, onion, garlic, leek, thyme sprigs, and rosemary. Season with a pinch of salt, then cook for about 15 minutes until softened.

2 Meanwhile, add the walnuts to a small skillet set over low-medium heat. Cook for about 3 minutes until the smell is nutty, then remove from the pan, roughly chop, and set aside.

3 Add the chickpeas and stock to the saucepan, then bring to a boil. Reduce the heat to low and cook for a further 5 minutes.

4 Add the lemon juice to the pan, then season with salt and freshly ground black pepper and blend with an immersion blender until smooth.

5 Divide among bowls and top with the walnuts, dill, and chili flakes.

Keep it This can be frozen for up to 3 months.

Fennel contains the phytochemical anethole, which stimulates digestive juices, aiding digestion.

Pork Meatballs with Lentils

Kcals 681
Protein 46g
Fiber 11g

Serves 4

Prep + cook time:
1 hour 30 minutes

- ¼ cup (30g) pine nuts
- ½ cup (70g) golden raisins
- 1 cup (50g) fresh whole wheat bread crumbs
- ⅓ cup (100ml) milk
- 1lb 2oz (500g) ground pork
- large handful of flat-leaf parsley, finely chopped
- grated zest of 1 lemon
- 2 tsp fennel seeds
- 2 tsp ground cinnamon
- 1 tbsp dried oregano
- 1 egg
- salt and freshly ground black pepper
- 2 tbsp extra-virgin olive oil
- steamed broccolini, to serve

Lentils:

- 1 tbsp extra-virgin olive oil
- 1 onion, finely chopped
- 2 cloves of garlic, crushed
- ⅓ cup (100ml) white wine
- 1 cup (200g) Puy lentils
- 3¼ cups (800ml) beef stock
- juice of 1 lemon
- handful of chives, finely chopped

1 To one bowl, add the pine nuts and golden raisins, cover with water, and let soak for 10–20 minutes. To another bowl, add the bread crumbs and milk, and let soak for 10–15 minutes.

2 To a large bowl, add the pork, parsley, lemon zest, fennel seeds, cinnamon, oregano, and egg. Drain the nuts and golden raisins, then add to the bowl. Squeeze the milk from the bread, then add the bread to the bowl. Season. Shape into 12 balls.

3 Add the olive oil to a large skillet set over medium-high heat. Once hot, add the meatballs and cook for 8 minutes, turning often, until golden and cooked through. Set aside.

4 For the lentils, add the olive oil to a saucepan and set over medium heat. Add the onion and fry for 5 minutes until softened. Add the garlic and cook for 1 minute. Add the wine and let it reduce by half. Add in the Puy lentils and beef stock, then bring to a boil. Once boiling, reduce to low heat. Cover and cook for 30 minutes until tender. Add the lemon juice, season, and top with the chives.

5 Serve the meatballs and lentils with broccolini.

Lean pork is a good source of low-fat protein and B vitamins.

Eggplant Ragù with Bean Mash

Kcals 529
Protein 23g
Fiber 19g

Serves 4

Prep + cook time:
1 hour, plus soaking time

- ¾ cup (100g) walnut halves or cashews
- 3 eggplants
- 2 tbsp extra-virgin olive oil, divided
- 1 onion, finely chopped
- 1 stalk of celery, finely chopped
- 1 carrot, peeled and finely chopped
- 2 cloves of garlic, crushed
- 1 tbsp paprika
- 7oz (200g) shiitake mushrooms, finely chopped
- 1 tbsp tomato paste
- 1¾ cups (400ml) passata
- 2 cups (500ml) vegetable stock
- ½ cup (100g) black or green dried lentils
- 1 tbsp balsamic vinegar
- salt and freshly ground black pepper
- 2 x 15.5oz (439g) cans of lima beans, drained and rinsed
- juice of ½ lemon

To serve (optional):

- chopped parsley
- grated Parmesan cheese

1 Add the nuts to a small bowl, cover with water, and let soak for 2 hours, or overnight. Drain, and blend to coarse crumbs in a blender. Set aside.

2 Pierce the eggplant skins all over. Cook them directly over the open flame on the stove, turning regularly, for 10 minutes until blistered and softened. Alternatively, put them onto a large baking sheet and cook in the oven for 45 minutes at 425°F (220°C) until collapsed.

3 Put the eggplants into a bowl, cover with plastic wrap, and leave for 10 minutes, then remove and discard the skins, chop the flesh, and set aside.

4 Heat 1 tablespoon oil in a large high-sided skillet over low-medium heat and cook the onion, celery, and carrot for 10 minutes until softened. Add the garlic, paprika, mushrooms, and eggplants and cook for 10 minutes. Add the tomato paste, passata, and stock. Bring to the boil, then reduce the heat to low, add the lentils, and cook for about 15 minutes until tender. Add the balsamic vinegar, then season with salt and freshly ground black pepper.

5 Meanwhile, add the remaining tablespoon of olive oil to a saucepan. Add the lima beans and warm through for a few minutes. Add the lemon juice and gently mash with a potato masher.

6 Serve the bean mash with the ragù, and sprinkle over parsley and Parmesan cheese, if you like.

Keep it This will keep in the fridge for up to 4 days or in the freezer for up to 3 months.

Smoky Slow-Cooked Beef Soup

Kcals 349
Protein 32g
Fiber 8g

Serves 6

Prep + cook time: 3 hours 30 minutes

- 1 x 14oz (400g) can of roma tomatoes
- 1 tbsp extra-virgin olive oil
- 1lb 5oz (600g) beef shank, cut into large chunks
- 1 onion, finely chopped
- 3 cloves of garlic, crushed
- 1 tbsp chipotle en adobo
- 1 tbsp smoked paprika
- 2 cups (500ml) pomegranate juice
- 2 cups (500ml) beef or chicken stock
- 6 beets, peeled and cut into 1¼in (3cm) chunks
- 2 x 14oz (400g) cans of lima beans, drained and rinsed
- 10½oz (300g) Swiss chard, stems finely chopped, leaves left whole
- juice of 1 lemon
- salt and freshly ground black pepper
- ½ cup (100g) Greek yogurt

1 Blend the tomatoes in a blender. Set aside.

2 Add the oil to a large ovenproof saucepan set over high heat. Once hot, brown the beef, in batches, on all sides. Remove and set aside.

3 Turn down to low heat, add the onion and garlic, and cook for 5 minutes until softened. Add the chipotle en adobo and paprika, and cook for a further 30 seconds.

4 Add the beef back into the pan, along with the pomegranate juice, stock, and beets. Cover and cook for 2 hours, then add the lima beans and cook for 1 hour more until the beef is tender and falling apart.

5 Add the chard stalks and cook for 3 minutes, then add the chard leaves and lemon juice. Stir through until the chard leaves have just wilted. Season with salt and freshly ground black pepper.

6 Divide among bowls and top with the yogurt.

Keep it This will keep in the fridge for up to 5 days or in the freezer for 3 months.

Canned tomatoes are a source of lycopene, which could help reduce the risk of heart disease.

Chana Dal

Kcals	337
Protein	18g
Fiber	10g

Makes 4

Prep + cook time:
1 hour 20 minutes, plus soaking time

- 1⅓ cups (250g) chana dal, rinsed and soaked for 3 hours
- 8 cups (2 liters) water
- 1 cinnamon stick
- 1 tsp ground turmeric, divided
- 4 green cardamom pods, bashed
- salt
- 2 tbsp (30g) butter or ghee
- 1 onion, finely chopped
- 2 cloves of garlic, crushed
- 1¼ in (3 cm) piece of ginger, peeled and finely chopped
- 2 tsp ground cumin
- 1 tsp ground coriander
- 2 tsp garam masala
- ½ tsp chili powder
- 1 x 14oz (411g) can of roma tomatoes

To serve (optional):

- Greek yogurt
- cilantro, roughly chopped

1 Add the chana dal into a large saucepan and cover with around 8 cups (2 liters) water. Add in the cinnamon stick, ½ teaspoon turmeric, and the cardamon pods. Season with salt, then bring to a boil. Once boiling, turn the heat down to low and cook for 1 hour until the lentils are tender.

2 Meanwhile, add the butter or ghee to a saucepan set over low-medium heat. Once hot, add the onion and cook for 10 minutes until softened.

3 Add in the garlic and ginger, then cook for a further minute until fragrant. Add the remaining ½ teaspoon turmeric, along with the cumin, coriander, garam masala, and chili powder. Cook for 30 seconds, then add the tomatoes and cook for about 20 minutes until the sauce looks thick and reduced. Season, then set aside.

4 Drain the lentils, then add to the skillet. Season with salt and serve with some yogurt topped with chopped cilantro, if liked.

5 Keep it This will keep in the freezer for up to 3 months.

Chana dal boasts impressive fiber and protein quantities, making it a real nutritional powerhouse to have on hand in the freezer.

Bean Chili

Kcals 612
Protein 27g
Fiber 24.5g

Serves 4

Prep + cook time: 35 minutes

- 2 tbsp extra-virgin olive oil
- 1 onion, finely chopped
- 4 cloves of garlic, crushed
- 1 red pepper, roughly chopped
- 1 green pepper, roughly chopped
- 1 tbsp tomato paste
- 1 tbsp ground cumin
- 1 tbsp smoked paprika
- 1 tbsp chipotle en adobo
- 1 tbsp dried oregano
- 1 tsp chili powder
- 2 x 15.5oz (439g) cans of kidney beans, drained and rinsed
- 1 x 15oz (425g) can of black beans, drained and rinsed
- 2 x 14.5oz (411g) cans of diced tomatoes
- 1¼ cups (300ml) vegetable stock
- salt and freshly ground black pepper
- 2 x 9oz (250g) pouches of microwaveable brown basmati rice
- 3 tbsp sour cream
- ½ cup (50g) grated Cheddar cheese
- handful of cilantro, roughly chopped

1 Add the olive oil to a large high-sided skillet set over low-medium heat. Add the onion, garlic, and both peppers, then cook for 5 minutes until softened.

2 Add in the tomato paste, cumin, paprika, chipotle en adobo, oregano, and chili powder, then cook for 1 minute.

3 Add in the canned beans, diced tomatoes, and vegetable stock, then season with salt and freshly ground black pepper. Cook for about 25 minutes, until the sauce has reduced.

4 Microwave the rice pouches according to the package instructions. Divide the rice and chili among plates and top with the sour cream, Cheddar cheese, and chopped cilantro.

Keep it This will keep in the fridge for up to 5 days or in the freezer for 3 months.

Red kidney beans and black beans provide B vitamins and iron. Like other beans and pulses, they are a good source of fiber, particularly soluble fiber.

Nut Roast

Kcals 505
Protein 20g
Fiber 6.5g

Makes 4

Prep + cook time:
1 hour

- ½oz (15g) dried porcini mushrooms
- ⅓ cup (100ml) boiling water
- 2 tbsp extra-virgin olive oil
- 1 onion, finely chopped
- 2 cloves of garlic, crushed
- 1 carrot, finely chopped
- 1 stalk of celery, finely chopped
- 3½oz (100g) brown button mushrooms, finely chopped
- 2 sprigs of rosemary, finely chopped
- salt and freshly ground black pepper
- ¾ cup (100g) mixed nuts (such as walnuts, hazelnuts, and pistachios), finely chopped
- 2 tbsp (20g) dried apricots, finely chopped
- 3 cups (150g) fresh bread crumbs
- 1 cup cooked lentils
- 1 x 6oz (250g) microwaveable pouch of chestnuts
- ⅓ cup (100ml) vegetable stock
- 2 eggs, beaten

1 Put the porcini mushrooms in a small bowl, add the boiling water, and set aside for 15 minutes.

2 Preheat the oven to 375°F (190°C) and line a 9 x 5in loaf pan with parchment paper.

3 Add the olive oil to a large skillet set over medium heat. Once hot, add the onion, garlic, carrot, celery, brown button mushrooms, and rosemary. Season, then cook for 10 minutes, until softened.

4 Meanwhile, drain the porcini mushrooms, keeping the liquid, and finely chop. Add the porcini mushrooms and their liquid to the pan.

5 Add in the nuts, apricots, bread crumbs, lentils, chestnuts, stock, and eggs. Season with salt and freshly ground black pepper and mix well. Put the mixture into the loaf pan, and press it down well.

6 Cover tightly with aluminum foil, then cook in the oven for 25 minutes. Remove the foil and cook for a further 20 minutes, until firm to the touch. Cool in the pan for 10 minutes, then remove from the pan, slice, and serve.

Keep it This nut roast will freeze well for up to 3 months.

Walnuts a rich in omega-3s, while pistachios contain calcium.

Air Fryer

An air fryer can be a handy piece of equipment when following a high-fiber diet, as it cuts down cooking time, allowing you to still opt for healthy, fiber-packed meals when you're in a hurry.

Masala Nut Mix

Kcals	197
Protein	6g
Fiber	2g

Serves 6

Prep + cook time: 10 minutes

- 1⅔ cups (200g) mixed nuts (such as cashews, almonds, unsalted peanuts, or pecans)
- 2 tbsp pumpkin seeds
- ½ tsp ground turmeric
- 1 tsp cayenne pepper
- 1 tsp garam masala
- 1 tsp ground cumin
- ½ tsp garlic powder
- ½ tsp salt
- 2 tbsp vegetable oil
- ½ tsp sugar

1 Preheat the air fryer to 325°F (160°C) for 3 minutes.

2 Add the nuts and seeds to a bowl, then add the turmeric, cayenne pepper, garam masala, cumin, garlic powder, salt, and vegetable oil. Mix well.

3 Add to the air fryer basket and cook for 6 minutes until golden.

4 Sprinkle over the sugar, mix well, and serve.

Tip This is a great way to use up leftover nuts. Use a mix of whichever nuts you have in your pantry.

Nuts and seeds are a good source of fiber, protein, healthy fats, and minerals, making them a great choice for snacking.

Celery Root Fries

Kcals 337
Protein 3.5g
Fiber 10.5g

Serves 2

Prep + cook time: 20 minutes

- ½ celery root, peeled and cut into ¾ in (2 cm) batons
- 2 tbsp extra-virgin olive oil
- 3 tbsp mayonnaise
- 1 tsp whole grain mustard
- 2 tbsp finely chopped tarragon
- juice of ½ lemon
- salt and freshly ground black pepper

1 Preheat the air fryer to 375°F (190°C) for 3 minutes.

2 To a bowl, add the celery root and olive oil, then mix well and add to the air fryer basket. Cook for 15 minutes, shaking the basket halfway through.

3 Meanwhile, to a small bowl, add the mayonnaise, mustard, tarragon, and lemon juice. Season with salt and freshly ground black pepper, then serve with the celery root fries.

Serve it These celery root fries would work well alongside some burgers.

Celery root contains both soluble and insoluble fiber, as well as boasting impressive amounts of vitamin K, which is important for strong, healthy bones.

Broccoli and Chickpea Salad

Kcals 528
Protein 22g
Fiber 18.5g

Serves 2

Prep + cook time:
25 minutes

- 1 x 15oz (425g) can of chickpeas, drained and rinsed
- 1 head of broccoli, cut into florets
- 2 tbsp canola oil
- 1 tsp sesame oil
- 1 tbsp soy sauce
- juice of 1 lime
- 2 tsp maple syrup or honey
- 1 clove of garlic, crushed
- ⅓ cup (40g) almonds, roughly chopped
- 1 red chile, finely chopped
- handful of mint, roughly chopped
- handful of cilantro, roughly chopped
- 2 tbsp pomegranate seeds
- 1 tbsp sesame seeds
- olive oil spray

1 Preheat the air fryer to 400°F (200°C) for 3 minutes.

2 Pat the chickpeas dry with paper towel or a clean kitchen towel, then add to the air fryer basket. Spray with some oil, then cook for 10 minutes, shaking the basket every 3 minutes, until golden and crispy. Remove and set aside.

3 Add the broccoli to the air fryer basket, spray with some oil, and cook for 5 minutes until softened and charred in places. Remove and set aside.

4 Meanwhile, to a small bowl, add the canola oil, sesame oil, soy sauce, lime juice, maple syrup or honey, and garlic. Whisk well, then set aside.

5 To a large bowl, add the chickpeas, broccoli, almonds, chile, mint, cilantro, and pomegranate seeds. Drizzle over the dressing, then mix well. Sprinkle over the sesame seeds and serve.

Serve it This would go well alongside some simply cooked chicken or fish, and even enjoyed on its own for a lunch or light dinner.

Chickpeas, like all beans and pulses, are rich in fiber and complex carbohydrates, which provide a slow, steady release of energy.

Chipotle Corn Riblets with Broccolini

Kcals	497
Protein	16g
Fiber	8g

Serves 2

Prep + cook time: 20 minutes

4 corn cobs
1 tbsp smoked paprika
1 tbsp ground cumin
1 tbsp chipotle powder
1 tbsp dried oregano
2 tbsp extra-virgin olive oil
salt and freshly ground black pepper
7oz (200g) broccolini
1 tbsp chipotle en adobo
2 tbsp mayonnaise
2 tbsp sour cream
1¾oz (50g) feta
handful of cilantro, roughly chopped
1 red chile, thinly sliced into rounds
lime wedges, to serve

1 Preheat the air fryer to 400°F (200°C) for 3 minutes.

2 Cook the corn in the microwave for 1 minute to soften slightly.

3 Using a sharp knife, trim the ends of the corn. Stand them up vertically and cut down through the middle of the core to halve each corn cob, being very careful. Cut each half again through the core to create quarters (though you can just cut into halves if you prefer).

4 Put the riblets into a large bowl and add the paprika, cumin, chipotle powder, oregano, and oil. Season with salt and freshly ground black pepper, then mix well until fully coated.

5 Put the riblets into the air fryer and cook for 5 minutes, then add in the broccolini and cook for a further 5 minutes until the riblets have curled and the edges are starting to crisp, and the broccolini is tender.

6 Meanwhile, to a small bowl, add the chipotle en adobo, mayo, and sour cream. Mix well, then set aside.

7 Arrange the corn riblets and broccolini on a platter. Drizzle over the chipotle sauce, crumble over the feta, then sprinkle over the cilantro and red chile. Serve with lime wedges on the side.

Serve it These corn riblets make a perfect air-fried snack or would also work well as part of a bigger Mexican spread.

Broccolini provides vitamins C and K, fiber, and phytochemicals called glucosinolates, which help reduce the risk of certain types of cancer.

Sweet Potato Wedges

Kcals	391
Protein	4g
Fiber	10g

Serves 2

Prep + cook time: 20 minutes

- 3 sweet potatoes, cut into wedges
- 1 tbsp onion powder
- 1 tbsp garlic powder
- 1 tbsp harissa
- 2 tbsp vegetable oil
- salt and freshly ground black pepper
- 2 green onions, finely chopped
- handful of chives, finely chopped
- sour cream, to serve

1 Preheat the air fryer to 350°F (180°C) for 3 minutes.

2 To a bowl, add the sweet potatoes, onion powder, garlic powder, harissa, and vegetable oil. Mix well, then add to the air fryer basket.

3 Cook for 15 minutes, shaking the basket halfway through. Season with salt and freshly ground black pepper.

4 Sprinkle over the green onions and chives, and serve with the sour cream.

Serve it These would work well with steak or fish.

Adding a little fat when you cook sweet potatoes makes it easier for your body to absorb the beta-carotene they contain.

Hispi Cabbage Pakoras

Kcals	58
Protein	3g
Fiber	3g

Makes 8

Prep + cook time: 20 minutes

½ hispi or Napa cabbage, shredded
1 carrot, grated
1 onion, thinly sliced
¾in (2 cm) piece of ginger, finely grated
1 clove of garlic, crushed
¼ tsp ground turmeric
1 tsp garam masala
½ tsp chili powder
1 green chile, seeded and finely chopped
2 tbsp cilantro, leaves roughly chopped and stalks finely chopped
salt
2 tbsp chickpea flour
vegetable or olive oil spray

To serve:
mango chutney
lime wedges

1 Preheat the air fryer to 375°F (190°C) for 3 minutes.

2 In a bowl, combine the cabbage, carrot, onion, ginger, garlic, turmeric, garam masala, chili powder, green chile, cilantro leaves and stalks, and a pinch of salt.

3 Add the chickpea flour to the bowl and mix well until combined. Add 2–3 tablespoons of water, bit by bit, just enough so that it clings together, making sure it is not overly wet.

4 Divide the mixture into eight portions and shape into loose balls. Put into the air fryer basket, spray generously with oil, and cook for 5 minutes. Spray with more oil, and cook for a further 5 minutes until golden.

5 Serve with mango chutney and lime wedges.

Swap it This pakora recipe can also be made with other vegetables, such as leeks.

Hispi cabbage is not only a great source of fiber, but also of vitamin C, which supports the immune system.

Cannellini Bean and Leek Gratin

Kcals 741
Protein 26g
Fiber 10.5g

Serves 4

Prep + cook time: 45 minutes

- 2 leeks, trimmed and sliced
- 2 cloves of garlic, thinly sliced
- 3 sprigs of thyme, leaves picked, plus extra to serve
- 2 tbsp extra-virgin olive oil
- salt
- ¼ cup (70ml) vegetable stock
- ⅓ cup (100ml) heavy cream
- 2 tbsp crème fraîche
- 1 tsp Dijon mustard
- 3¼ cups (600g) canned cannellini beans, drained
- 2 cups (200g) grated Cheddar cheese
- 1½ cups (80g) fresh bread crumbs
- vegetable or olive oil spray

1 Preheat the air fryer to 325°F (160°C) for 3 minutes.

2 In a dish that fits in the air fryer, put the leeks, garlic, and thyme. Drizzle over the olive oil and season with a little salt. Cook for 12 minutes until the leeks have softened.

3 Add in the vegetable stock, heavy cream, crème fraîche, Dijon mustard, and cannellini beans. Mix well, and cook at 340°F (170°C) for 12 minutes until the sauce slightly thickens.

4 Sprinkle over the Cheddar cheese and bread crumbs, spray with some oil, then cook at 375°F (190°C) for 15 minutes until the sauce is bubbling and the bread crumbs are golden. Serve topped with extra thyme.

Keep it This gratin can be made in advance, then reheated when ready to serve.

Leeks are high in antioxidants, which have anti-inflammatory properties and reduce the risk of certain cancers.

Spiced Cod with Bombay Potatoes

Kcals 715
Protein 38g
Fiber 18g

Serves 2

Prep + cook time: 30 minutes

- 4 sweet potatoes, cut into 1¾ in (4 cm) cubes
- 1 tbsp ground cumin
- 1 tsp ground coriander
- 1 tsp ground turmeric, divided
- 1 tsp chili powder, divided
- 2 tbsp vegetable oil, divided
- salt and freshly ground black pepper
- 7oz (200g) broccolini
- 1 tbsp garam masala
- 1 tsp garlic powder
- 1 tsp onion powder
- juice of 2 lemons, divided
- 2 x 5oz (150g) cod fillets
- ⅓ cup (100g) Greek yogurt
- large handful of mint
- 3 tbsp pomegranate seeds

Cod is an excellent source of protein while being extremely low in fat.

1 Preheat the air fryer to 350°F (180°C) for 3 minutes.

2 To a bowl, add the sweet potatoes, cumin, ground coriander, ½ teaspoon turmeric, ½ teaspoon chili powder, and 1 tablespoon vegetable oil. Season with salt and freshly ground black pepper, then put into the air fryer basket and cook for 6 minutes at 350°F (180°C). Shake the basket, add the broccolini, and cook for 6 minutes more. Remove from the air fryer and set aside.

3 To a baking dish that fits in the air fryer, add the remaining oil, turmeric, and chili powder, along with the garam masala, garlic powder, onion powder, and the juice of 1 lemon. Add the fish, and turn in the marinade until fully coated. Season with salt and freshly ground black pepper, then cook at 340°F (170°C) for 7 minutes until cooked through.

4 Meanwhile, to a small bowl, add the yogurt, most of the mint, and the remaining lemon juice. Season with salt and freshly ground black pepper, then set aside.

5 Divide the potatoes, cod, and broccolini between plates and add the yogurt. Sprinkle over the remaining mint and the pomegranate seeds, and serve.

Swap it Other fish such as salmon or sea bass would work well here.

Sweet and Sour Tofu

Kcals 484
Protein 21g
Fiber 7.5g

Serves 4

Prep + cook time: 20 minutes

- 1lb (450g) firm tofu
- 1 tsp garlic powder
- 3 tbsp cornstarch
- vegetable oil spray
- 1 yellow pepper
- 1 green pepper
- 1 onion, sliced
- ¼ pineapple, cored and cut into 1¾ in (4 cm) cubes
- ⅔ cup (150ml) pineapple juice
- 2 tbsp soy sauce
- 1 tbsp sweet chili sauce
- 1 tbsp light brown sugar
- 1 tbsp rice wine vinegar
- 2 tbsp water
- 2 x 9oz (250g) pouches of microwaveable brown basmati rice
- 1 tbsp sesame seeds
- 2 green onions, thinly sliced

1 Preheat the air fryer to 400°F (200°C) for 3 minutes.

2 Pat the tofu dry and cut into ¾in (2cm) cubes. Add to a bowl with the garlic powder and 2½ tablespoons cornstarch. Mix well and add to the air fryer basket. Spray liberally with oil, cook at 400°F (200°C) for 10 minutes until crispy, then remove and set aside.

3 Deseed and roughly chop the peppers, then add to a dish that fits in the air fryer, along with the onion and pineapple. Spray with some oil, then cook at 350°F (180°C) for 7 minutes until softened.

4 Meanwhile, add the pineapple juice, soy sauce, sweet chili sauce, brown sugar, and rice wine vinegar to a small saucepan over medium heat.

5 Add the remaining ½ tablespoon cornstarch to a small bowl with the 2 tablespoons water. Mix to a slurry, then stir into the sauce. Cook the sauce to a thick consistency, then set aside.

6 Add the tofu to the dish with the vegetables, pour in the sauce, and cook in the air fryer at 350°F (180°C) for 3 minutes.

7 Meanwhile, microwave the rice pouches according to the package instructions.

8 Divide the rice and sweet and sour tofu among plates, sprinkle over the sesame seeds and green onions, and serve.

Pineapples and pineapple juice contain an enzyme called bromelain, which helps break down protein in food, making it easier to digest.

Chicken Shawarma Hummus Bowl

Kcals	655
Protein	51g
Fiber	12g

Serves 3

Prep + cook time: 35 minutes, plus marinating time

- 5 boneless chicken thighs
- 1 tsp dried oregano
- 2 tsp smoked paprika
- 2 tsp ground cumin
- 1 tsp garlic powder
- ¼ cup (60g) Greek yogurt
- 1 tbsp extra-virgin olive oil
- grated zest and juice of 1 lemon
- salt and freshly ground black pepper
- ½ red onion, thinly sliced
- 1 cup (200g) hummus
- 3½oz (100g) roasted red peppers, thinly sliced
- ¼ red cabbage, shredded
- 3½oz (100g) cherry tomatoes, halved
- ¼ cucumber, diced
- handful of flat-leaf parsley, roughly chopped
- 3 whole wheat pitas

1 To a bowl, add the chicken, oregano, paprika, cumin, garlic powder, Greek yogurt, olive oil, and lemon zest. Season with salt and freshly ground black pepper, then mix well and marinate for 1 hour, or overnight.

2 Preheat the air fryer to 350°F (180°C) for 3 minutes.

3 Skewer the chicken thighs, add to the air fryer basket, and cook for 30 minutes until cooked through and charred in places. Slice and set aside.

4 Meanwhile, add the red onion to a small bowl, squeeze over the lemon juice, and season with a little salt. Scrunch together with your hands, then set aside to pickle.

5 To serve, divide the hummus among bowls. Top with the chicken, red peppers, cabbage, tomatoes, cucumber, parsley, and pickled red onion. Season with salt and freshly ground black pepper, and add the pita breads.

Whole wheat pitas contain twice as much fibre as white pitas.

Chicken Schnitzel with Sweet Potato Fries and Celery Root Remoulade

Kcals 826
Protein 53g
Fiber 20g

Serves 2

Prep + cook time: 30 minutes

- 2 chicken breasts
- 2 tbsp all-purpose flour
- 2 eggs
- 2 cups (100g) fresh whole wheat bread crumbs
- salt and freshly ground black pepper
- 2 sweet potatoes, peeled and cut into batons
- 1 tbsp vegetable oil
- 1 tbsp smoked paprika
- vegetable oil spray

Celery root remoulade:

- ½ celery root, peeled and cut into thin matchsticks
- 1 green apple, cored and cut into thin matchsticks
- 2 tbsp mayonnaise
- 1 tbsp crème fraîche
- 1 tbsp whole grain mustard
- juice of 1 lemon
- handful of chives, finely chopped

To serve:

- lemon wedges
- mayonnaise

1 Preheat the air fryer to 400°F (200°C) for 3 minutes.

2 Slice the chicken breasts lengthwise, not quite cutting all the way through, then open out like a book. Cover with plastic wrap and bash with a rolling pin until ½ in (1 cm) thick.

3 Put the flour, eggs, and bread crumbs into three separate small dishes. Whisk the eggs well, and add a pinch of salt to the flour.

4 Coat each chicken breast first in the flour, then the eggs, and finally the bread crumbs.

5 Add the chicken to the air fryer basket, spray liberally with oil, and cook for 12 minutes, flipping halfway through. Remove and set aside.

6 Meanwhile, add the sweet potatoes to a bowl, drizzle over the oil, sprinkle over the paprika, and season with salt and freshly ground black pepper. Add to the air fryer basket, then cook at 350°F (180°C) for 10 minutes, shaking halfway through.

7 Meanwhile, combine the remoulade ingredients in a bowl and season to taste.

8 Serve the chicken, sweet potato fries, and remoulade with lemon wedges and mayonnaise.

Bean Burgers

Kcals 420
Protein 21g
Fiber 7g

Serves 4

Prep + cook time: 20 minutes

- 1 x 15oz (400g) can lima beans, drained and rinsed
- 1 zucchini, grated
- 2 cups (100g) panko bread crumbs
- 1 red onion, ½ finely chopped and ½ sliced
- 2 cloves of garlic, crushed
- 1 tbsp ground cumin
- ½ tsp cayenne pepper
- 1 egg
- handful of cilantro, leaves roughly chopped and stalks finely chopped
- salt and freshly ground black pepper
- 4 burger buns
- 2 Little Gem lettuces, leaves separated
- 4 slices of American cheese
- vegetable or olive oil spray

To serve:

- mayonnaise
- ketchup

1 Preheat the air fryer to 350°F (180°C) for 3 minutes.

2 In a bowl, mash the beans with a fork. Add in the zucchini, bread crumbs, chopped red onion, garlic, cumin, cayenne pepper, egg, and cilantro leaves and stalks. Season well with salt and freshly ground black pepper.

3 Shape into four burger patties and put into the air fryer basket. Spray with some oil, then cook for 10 minutes. Turn the patties over, spray with a little more oil, and cook for a further 5 minutes until golden in color.

4 Meanwhile, toast the burger buns.

5 To assemble, spread mayo on the base of the burger buns, then add a couple of lettuce leaves. Add a bean burger patty on top, a slice of cheese, and some sliced red onion. Finish with ketchup on the burger lid.

Keep it These burgers can be frozen for up to 3 months.

Swap it Substitute the beans for chickpeas or kidney beans.

Lima beans contribute to lowering the body's cholesterol levels, reducing the chance of illnesses, including heart disease.

Snacks & Sweets

These snacks and sweets are designed to keep you feeling full while quelling any cravings. Whether it's something sweet or savory you're after, this chapter has just what you might fancy for guilt-free snacking.

Seeded Crackers with Artichoke Dip

Kcals 635
Protein 23g
Fiber 13g

Serves 2

Prep + cook time: 50 minutes

- ½ cup (50g) rye flour
- ½ cup (75g) all-purpose flour, plus extra for dusting
- 3 tbsp canola oil, divided
- 2 tsp fennel seeds
- 1 tbsp sesame seeds
- 2 tbsp nigella seeds
- 1 tbsp sunflower seeds
- 1 tsp salt
- 4½ tbsp water
- 1½ cups (250g) canned cannellini beans, drained
- 3 tbsp Greek yogurt
- 2 tbsp sour cream
- 1 tsp Dijon mustard
- 1 clove of garlic
- juice of ½ lemon
- salt and freshly ground black pepper
- 5¼oz (150g) spinach
- 6½oz (185g) jarred artichokes, drained
- ½ cup (50g) each grated Cheddar and Gruyère cheese

Rinsing beans before you use them will help reduce the sugars that can cause bloating.

1 Preheat the oven to 400°F (200°C). Line a baking sheet and set aside.

2 To a bowl, add both of the flours, 2 tablespoons canola oil, the fennel seeds, sesame seeds, nigella seeds, sunflower seeds, salt, and water. Mix together, then knead for 1 minute, using a little extra flour as needed, until smooth.

3 Once smooth, divide the dough into eight pieces. Roll out as thin as you can, and transfer to the lined baking sheet. You may need to do this in batches. Cook in the oven for 12 minutes until golden, then let cool.

4 Meanwhile, to a blender, add the cannellini beans, Greek yogurt, sour cream, Dijon mustard, garlic, and lemon juice. Season with salt and freshly ground black pepper, then blend until smooth. Transfer to a small baking dish. Roughly chop the spinach, then add to the baking dish along with the artichokes, Cheddar cheese, and half of the Gruyère cheese. Mix well, then top with the remaining Gruyère.

5 Bake for 25–30 minutes until golden and bubbling. Serve the dip alongside the crackers.

Keep it These crackers will keep in an airtight container for up to 2 weeks.

Pumpkin Croquettes

Kcals 248
Protein 9g
Fiber 2g

Serves 4

Prep + cook time:
45 minutes, plus chilling time

- 1lb 2oz (500g) pumpkin or butternut squash, peeled and cut into large chunks
- pinch of nutmeg
- 3 tbsp all-purpose flour, divided
- salt and freshly ground black pepper
- 2 eggs
- 2 cups (100g) panko bread crumbs
- vegetable oil spray

Sauce:

- 2 tbsp ketchup
- ¾ in (2 cm) piece of ginger, peeled and finely chopped
- 1 clove of garlic, crushed
- 1 tbsp Worcestershire sauce
- 1 tbsp soy sauce
- 1 tsp oyster sauce
- 2 tsp dark brown sugar
- 1 tsp maple syrup or honey

1 Fill a large saucepan halfway with water and set over medium heat. Once simmering, set a steamer basket or colander over it. Add the pumpkin or squash, cover with a lid, and cook for 10 minutes until completely softened.

2 Transfer the pumpkin or squash to a bowl, then mash with a potato masher or fork until smooth. Add in the nutmeg and 2 tablespoons flour, then season with salt and freshly ground black pepper. Mix well, then chill for 1 hour to firm up.

3 Preheat the oven to 425°F (220°C).

4 Put the remaining 1 tablespoon flour, eggs, and bread crumbs into three separate small dishes. Whisk the eggs well, and add a pinch of salt to the flour.

5 Take a tablespoon of the pumpkin mixture and roll it into a ball. Repeat with all the mixture, lining the balls up onto a large baking sheet as you go.

6 Coat each pumpkin ball in the flour, then the eggs, and finally the bread crumbs until fully coated, then place back onto the baking sheet.

7 Spray the croquettes liberally with oil, then put into the oven and cook for 20 minutes until golden and crispy.

8 Meanwhile, combine all of the ingredients for the sauce in a bowl.

9 Serve the croquettes with the sauce.

Keep it These would freeze well for up to 3 months.

Pumpkin and butternut squash are rich in beta-carotene, which the body can convert into vitamin A.

Corn Fritters

Kcals 228
Protein 8g
Fiber 5.5g

Serves 2

Prep + cook time: 15 minutes

- 1½ cups (200g) canned corn, drained
- 1 tbsp red Thai chili paste
- 2 green onions, finely chopped
- ½ in (1 cm) piece of ginger, peeled and finely chopped
- handful of cilantro, roughly chopped
- ⅓ cup (50g) chickpea flour
- ½ tsp baking powder
- salt and freshly ground black pepper
- 2 tbsp vegetable oil
- juice of 1 lime
- sriracha mayonnaise, to serve (optional)

1 To a bowl, add the corn, red Thai chili paste, green onions, ginger, cilantro, chickpea flour, and baking powder. Season with salt and freshly ground black pepper.

2 Add water, a tablespoon at a time, mixing between each addition, until the mixture is sticky but not runny, then set aside.

3 Add the oil to a skillet set over medium-high heat. Once hot, using a large spoon, scoop up some of the mixture, and gently add to the pan, pressing down to flatten. Cook for about 3 minutes on each side until golden. Remove from the pan and keep warm while you repeat with the remaining mixture.

4 Squeeze over the lime and serve with sriracha mayonnaise, if liked.

Keep it These fritters will keep in the freezer for up to 3 months.

Chickpea flour is made from chickpeas—it is a good alternative to wheat flour for people who can't eat gluten.

Granola Squares

Kcals 367
Protein 6.5g
Fiber 3g

Serves 8

Prep + cook time: 40 minutes

- ⅔ cup (150g) unsalted butter, plus extra for greasing
- ¼ cup (80g) maple syrup
- 2 cups (200g) old-fashioned rolled oats
- ¾ cup (100g) mixed seeds (such as pumpkin seeds, sunflower seeds, flaxseeds, or sesame seeds)
- ½ cup (60g) raisins

1 Preheat the oven to 350°F (180°C). Line an 8 in (20 cm) square pan with parchment paper and set aside.

2 Melt the butter and maple syrup in a saucepan set over low-medium heat. Add in the oats, seeds, and raisins, then stir until fully coated. Transfer to the pan, pressing the mixture down flat with the back of a large spoon.

3 Put into the oven and cook for 30 minutes until firm to touch and golden. Let cool in the pan, then turn out and cut into squares to serve.

Keep it These granola squares will freeze well for up to 3 months.

Oats come in different types. Steel-cut oats are digested more slowly than rolled oats, which will help you feel fuller for longer.

Black Bean Brownies

Kcals 626
Protein 14g
Fiber 7g

Serves 6

Prep + cook time: 35 minutes

- ⅔ cup (150g) unsalted butter, plus extra for greasing
- 5¼oz (150g) dark chocolate, roughly chopped
- 1 x 15oz (425g) can of black beans, drained and rinsed
- 3 eggs
- ¾ cup (150g) light brown sugar
- 1 tsp vanilla extract
- ¾ cup (80g) cocoa powder
- 3 tbsp hazelnuts, roughly chopped
- 3 tbsp pumpkin seeds

1 Preheat the oven to 375°F (190°C). Line an 8in (20cm) square pan with parchment paper and set aside.

2 Melt the butter in a small saucepan set over low-medium heat.

3 Add the chocolate to a heatproof bowl. Either microwave the chocolate in 10-second intervals until melted or set over a saucepan of simmering water (making sure the bottom of the bowl doesn't touch the water) until melted.

4 To a blender, add the black beans, melted butter, eggs, sugar, and vanilla extract. Blend until smooth, then transfer to a bowl. Add the cocoa powder and melted chocolate. Mix well until fully combined, then add to the prepared pan and smooth out evenly.

5 Top with the chopped hazelnuts and pumpkin seeds, then bake in the oven for 20–25 minutes until set.

6 Let cool in the pan, then turn out and slice to serve.

Keep it These freeze well for up to 3 months.

In addition to fiber and protein, pumpkin seeds provide useful amounts of vitamins B1 and B2, as well as the minerals zinc, magnesium, and iron.

Date and Tahini cookies

Kcals 557
Protein 8g
Fiber 5g

Makes 6

Prep + cook time: 25 minutes

- ⅔ cup (150g) unsalted butter
- 3 tbsp tahini
- 1 egg
- 2 tsp sesame oil
- 2 tbsp vanilla extract
- ¾ cup (100g) pitted dates, finely chopped
- ⅓ cup (50g) walnut halves, finely chopped
- ½ cup (100g) light brown sugar
- ⅓ cup (50g) all-purpose flour
- 50g (generous ⅓ cup) spelt flour
- 1 tsp baking soda
- 3 tbsp cocao nibs
- 2 tbsp sesame seeds

1 Preheat the oven to 375°F (190°C) and line a large baking sheet with parchment paper.

2 Add the butter to a small saucepan set over medium heat. Cook until the butter is melted, smells nutty, and you can see the milk solids start to brown. Remove from the heat and pour into a bowl.

3 Add in the tahini, egg, sesame oil, and vanilla extract. Whisk well, then add in the dates, walnuts, sugar, all-purpose flour, spelt flour, baking soda, and cocao nibs. Fold together until fully combined.

4 Spread the sesame seeds out onto a small baking sheet, then set aside.

5 Take a large spoonful of the mixture, roll it into a ball, then roll it in the sesame seeds to coat all over. Put onto the lined baking sheet, then repeat with the remaining mixture, making sure that the cookies are well spaced out on the baking sheet.

6 Cook for 15 minutes until the cookies are golden. Remove from the oven and push the cookies down flat with the back of a cup. Let cool completely on the baking sheet, then serve.

Swap it Swap the tahini for smooth peanut butter if you prefer.

In addition to fiber, tahini provides heart-friendly fats and the minerals calcium, iron, potassium, and zinc.

Carrot Cake Bites

Kcals	108
Protein	2g
Fiber	3g

Makes 10

Prep time: 15 minutes

- 4 carrots, grated
- 4 pitted dates
- 1 tbsp ground cinnamon
- 1 tbsp maple syrup
- ½ cup (50g) old-fashioned rolled oats
- ⅓ cup (50g) walnut halves
- ¼ tsp salt
- 3 tbsp shredded coconut

1 To a blender, add the grated carrots, dates, cinnamon, maple syrup, oats, walnuts, and salt. Blend until the mixture comes together.

2 Roll the mixture into 10 balls.

3 Add the shredded coconut to a small baking tray, then roll each ball in the coconut until fully coated.

Keep it Keep in the refrigerator for 5 days, or freeze for up to 3 months.

In addition to fiber, dates contain impressive amounts of potassium, which helps counteract the effect of too much salt in the diet. They also provide useful amounts of iron.

Mint Chocolate Chia Seed Pudding

Kcals	705
Protein	21g
Fiber	19g

Serves 2

Prep + cook time:
5 minutes, plus setting time

- 3oz (90g) dark chocolate, roughly chopped
- ¾ cup (100g) chia seeds
- handful of mint, roughly chopped
- 2 cups (500ml) milk of choice
- 2 tbsp maple syrup
- 1 tsp vanilla extract
- ¼ tsp salt
- handful of berries of choice

1 Add the chocolate to a heatproof bowl. Either microwave the chocolate in 10-second intervals until melted or set over a saucepan of simmering water (making sure the bottom of the bowl doesn't touch the water) until melted.

2 To a blender, add the chia seeds, mint, milk, maple syrup, vanilla extract, salt, and half the melted chocolate. Blend until smooth.

3 Pour the pudding into two glasses, then pour the remaining melted chocolate over the top. Put into the fridge for 2 hours to set.

4 Top with berries and serve.

Swap it This would also work well with orange or plain chocolate.

Dark chocolate contains a group of phytochemicals called flavonoids, which are believed to help improve blood flow to the brain.

Mixed Berry Crumble

Kcals 515
Protein 7.5g
Fiber 8.5g

Serves 8

Prep + cook time:
35 minutes

- ¾ cup (200g) cold unsalted butter, cut into cubes
- ¾ cup (100g) all-purpose flour
- ¾ cup (100g) whole wheat flour
- ¾ cup (150g) light brown sugar
- 1 cup (100g) old-fashioned rolled oats
- 6 tbsp (50g) flaxseeds
- 2½ tbsp (20g) pumpkin seeds
- 2¼lb (1kg) frozen berries
- 3 tbsp demerara sugar

1 Preheat the oven to 400°F (200°C).

2 To a large bowl, add the butter, both flours, sugar, oats, flaxseeds, and pumpkin seeds. Rub together with your fingers until you have large crumbs, then set aside.

3 Add the berries to a large baking dish, top with the crumble mixture, then sprinkle the demerara sugar over the top.

4 Bake in the oven for 25 minutes until golden in color, then serve.

Swap it Swap the berries for fruits of choice; apples would work well here.

Flaxseeds are a good source of fiber, with 1 tablespoon providing 3g of fiber. They also contain omega-3 fats, which help keep the heart and brain healthy.

Conversion Charts

MEASURES

North America, New Zealand, and the United Kingdom use a 5ml teaspoon and a 15ml tablespoon. North American measuring cups hold approximately 240ml. An Australian metric measuring cup holds approximately 250ml; one Australian metric tablespoon holds 20ml; one Australian metric teaspoon holds 5ml.

The difference between one country's measuring cups and another's is within a two- or three-teaspoon variance and will not affect your cooking results. All cup and spoon measurements are level.

The most accurate way of measuring dry ingredients is to weigh them.

When measuring liquids, use a clear glass or plastic measuring cup with markings. We use large eggs with an average weight of 60g each.

DRY MEASURES

metric	imperial
15g	½oz
30g	1oz
60g	2oz
90g	3oz
125g	4oz (¼lb)
155g	5oz
185g	6oz
220g	7oz
250g	8oz (½lb)
280g	9oz
315g	10oz
345g	11oz
375g	12oz (¾lb)
410g	13oz
440g	14oz
470g	15oz
500g	16oz (1lb)
750g	24oz (1½lb)
1kg	32oz (2lb)

LIQUID MEASURES

metric	imperial
30ml	1 fluid oz
60ml	2 fluid oz
100ml	3 fluid oz
125ml	4 fluid oz
150ml	5 fluid oz
190ml	6 fluid oz
250ml	8 fluid oz
300ml	10 fluid oz
500ml	16 fluid oz
600ml	20 fluid oz
1000ml (1 liter)	1 quart

LENGTH MEASURES

metric	imperial
3mm	⅛in
6mm	¼in
1cm	½in
2cm	¾in
2.5cm	1in
5cm	2in
6cm	2½in
8cm	3in
10cm	4in
13cm	5in
15cm	6in
18cm	7in
20cm	8in
22cm	9in
25cm	10in
28cm	11in
30cm	12in (1ft)

Index

Note: page numbers in **bold** refer to illustrations.

Q

R

S

About the authors

Susanna Unsworth is a chef, food stylist, and writer based in London. She trained at Leiths School of Food and Wine.

Fiona Hunter is a nutritionist, food writer, and broadcaster.

Publisher's acknowledgments

DK would like to thank Fiona Hunter for nutritional consultancy, Rudy Hemming for assistance with food styling, Kathryn Glendenning for proofreading, Renee Wilmeth for consulting on the US edition, and Lisa Footitt for providing the index.

DK LONDON

Editorial Director Cara Armstrong
Project Editor Izzy Holton
US Senior Editor Jennette ElNaggar
Senior Designer Jordan Lambley
Senior Production Controller Stephanie McConnell
DTP and Design Coordinator Heather Blagden
Art Director Maxine Pedliham
Publishing Director Stephanie Jackson

DK DELHI

Senior Art Editor Ira Sharma
Preproduction Designer Manish Upreti
Preproduction Image Editor Vijay Kandwar
Preproduction and DTP Coordinator Pushpak Tyagi
Preproduction Manager Balwant Singh
Preproduction Image Manager Pankaj Sharma
Creative Head Malavika Talukder

Author, Recipe Developer, & Food Stylist Susanna Unsworth
Editor Kate Reeves-Brown
Photographer Clare Winfield
Prop Stylist Charlie Phillips

First American Edition, 2026
Published in the United States by DK Publishing,
a division of Penguin Random House LLC
1745 Broadway, 20th Floor, New York, NY 10019

26 27 28 29 30 10 9 8 7 6 5 4 3 2 1
001–362133–June/2026

Published in Great Britain by Dorling Kindersley Limited

ISBN 979-8-2173-1028-9

Printed and bound in the United Kingdom

www.dk.com

This book was made with Forest Stewardship Council™ certified paper—one small step in DK's commitment to a sustainable future.
Learn more at www.dk.com/uk/information/sustainability